CW01650022

House Plants
for South Africa

House Plants
for South Africa

Keith Kirsten   Owen A. Reid

Human & Rousseau
Cape Town Pretoria

The publication of this book at a reasonable price has been made possible by a contribution from Braaks Indoor Plants, distributors of quality house plants in South Africa.

The eleven illustrations in the section on *Pests and problems* were specially commissioned and supplied by Efekto.

Copyright © 1988 by Keith Kirsten and Owen A. Reid
First published in 1988 by Human & Rousseau (Pty) Ltd
State House, 3-9 Rose Street, Cape Town
Atrium Building, 60 Glenwood Road, Pretoria
Photography by John Brunda, Nancy Gardiner, Rob Böck and C. Kunhardt
Colour illustrations on pp. 24, 25 and 26 by A. Ollewage
Illustrations on pp. 15, 27 and 71 by Robyn Arnold
Symbols designed by Debbie Odendaal
Typography and cover design by Etienne van Duyker
Typeset in 10 on 11 pt Palatino by Studiographix, Cape Town
Colour separations by Studiographix, Cape Town
Printed and bound by Printpak Books, Dacres Avenue, Epping

ISBN 0 7981 2325 7

No part of this book may be reproduced or transmitted in any form or by any means, electronic or mechanical, or by photocopying, recording or microfilming, or stored in any retrieval system, without the written permission of the publisher

Foreword

Growing house plants is my business and I am delighted to be able to write the foreword not only to a very beautiful book but one which I feel is very important in today's South African gardening context.

It has come at a time when the great outdoors of trees, shrubs and vines is shrinking rapidly before the onslaught of 'progress' and when gardeners are turning more and more to indoor gardening for wellbeing and inner tranquillity. Indoor gardening is one form of gardening everyone can enjoy, whether living on a large property, in a penthouse or in a single room.

With this in mind nurserymen, growers and biologists have teamed up to push back the frontiers of indoor gardening. They have augmented our knowledge of cultivating and breeding indoor flowering and foliage plants while developing an infinite range of new varieties, and in their beautifully illustrated book Keith and Owen have superbly captured the excitement of this form of home decoration.

I am particularly pleased at the inclusion of many indigenous plants, such as the lachenalias which have been developed locally into a breath-taking range of new and colourful varieties.

In this, the fifth book published by these two well-known gardening personalities, they have once again managed very simply and succinctly to provide all the information necessary for busy people to manage their house plants successfully. Most gratifying is the way in which they have had all the facts and recommendations checked by the growers of South Africa's top quality plants – the members of the Pot Plant Sector of the South African Nurserymen's Association.

For too long have we had to rely on books on specialist subjects from overseas and I must congratulate Keith and Owen for producing this much needed addition to our indigenous library of indoor gardening books. *House Plants for South Africa* is long overdue!

Elro G. Braak
Braaks Indoor Plants
Pretoria

Acknowledgements

We would like to thank the following people for all their help in making this book possible:

The Pot Plant Sector of the South African Nurserymen's Association. Their members not only provided much of the information for the book but also plants for photographing. They shared in the final selection of the house plants they consider most suitable for indoor culture in South Africa and, importantly, those they know to be generally available. In addition a panel of members – all experienced growers – checked each plant description for accuracy.

Pot Plant Sector members who deserve special thanks are: Mr. André Barnhoorn and Mr. Floris Barnhoorn (Hadeco Wholesale Flower-Bulb Growers); Mr. Peter Barnhoorn (Peba Houseplants); Mr. Billy Minne (Carmel Estate Nurseries); Mr. Hugo Proper (Florex Indoor Plant Service (Pty.) Ltd.); Mr. Michael Rana (Flora Farms); Mr. L. Saayman (LVG Potplants); Mr. John Thorpe (The Potted Plant – Interior Plantscapers); Mr. and Mrs. N. van Wyk (Tuberflora Nursery); Mr. Kuys Versteeg (Versteeg Pot Plant Nursery); Mr. Hybert van der Voerst (Impala Nursery (Pty.) Ltd.); Mr. Douglas Watson (Marketing Director) and the staff of Braaks Indoor Plants and Mr. Hans Wohlgensinger and Mrs. Marge Oberholzer (Roeloffs' Nurseries).

Specialist help was also given by: Mr. and Mrs. Stefan Ernst (Pretoria Cactus, Aloe and Succulent Nursery) – succulents and cactii; Mr. Wilfred Grey (Tropical Plants and Gardens (Pty.) Ltd.) – bromeliads; Dr. Jan Herholdt (Meillandina) – miniature roses; Mr. Rolf Rawe (Valhalla Research) – tillandsias and Mr. Bill Smit (Efekto) – pests and diseases.

Others who helped in a variety of ways are: Mrs. Adri Cloete (Rochelle Nursery); Mr. Eggidio Freitas (Exotica Nursery); Mrs. Mary Matthews, co-ordinator Plant Plan and the staffs of Keith Kirsten's Parktown North Nurseries and Waterkloof Garden Centre.

Contents

Introduction

'Knowledge' is synonymous with green fingers. There is no doubt that the more you learn about plants the greener your fingers become. With knowledge and experience anyone can grow indoor plants successfully, and the purpose of this book is to provide, in as simple and digestible a form as possible, details of how to go about it.

This is a book for the home owner, not necessarily even the home gardener, although we hope that readers will have sufficient success with their house plants to become gardening enthusiasts. We have written neither for specialists nor plant collectors, but have rather described indoor plant varieties which we believe may be grown successfully by practically anyone, even children. These plants are suited to our warm and sunny climate, and to growing in the South African home. We also know that they are generally available at most nurseries and garden centres throughout the country, for there are few things more frustrating than learning about a plant that appeals to you, only to discover that it is unobtainable. All the entries in our directory section have therefore been most carefully vetted, with a plant's availability being one of the main selection criteria.

We have included detailed descriptions of nearly 135 plants, plus their many varieties. They are illustrated with one or more gorgeous photographs, and we've often included close-ups of each plant's flowers and leaves, or any interesting texture or brilliant colour patterning it might display.

In order to provide the most up-to-date list of available plants, we have worked very closely with the Pot Plant Sector of the South African Nurserymen's Association – the actual growers of the plants – and as a result our directory includes a number of varieties not previously sold in South Africa. There is even a section on that unbelievably beautiful genus of veld flowers, the *Lachenalia*, which scientists at the Roodeplaat Vegetable and Ornamental Research Institute have only recently hybridised into a whole range of modern and many-coloured pot plants. These plants have just become available after eight or more years of intensive research.

Remember, new plants are being released all the time, so it is wise to talk to your local nurseryman to find out what is available. He will be happy to help you and to give you all the vital information you require about light requirements, watering and a feeding regimen.

There are undoubtedly many plants that will grow in the home but which we have not included because they are disappointing performers or because they require more effort and specialist knowledge than we believe the average home owner is prepared to spend on his indoor garden. There are also a great many plants from countries in the Northern Hemisphere which we have omitted because they are really not suited to our conditions and are not available here.

The plants we have included, though, are suitable for practically any position except in total darkness – and even then you may grow them using special lighting. Whatever your requirements, you will find the right plant at your local garden centre. Your plants may be used as accent or form plants, to create indoor jungles, for table tops, as room dividers, or allowed to grow into tall trees where boldness is required. Some look very beautiful, even hanging from the ceiling.

To cope with the different growing conditions, plants need to be tough. We have therefore chosen survivors. Not all of them will enjoy the many different conditions; each varies, and the big secret is to get the right plant for the right position, an area this book deals with extensively.

Today few people have the time to acquire knowledge, let alone delve for it. We have laid out our book in such a way that by the flick of a page you will be able to find all the information necessary to grow your particular plant choice successfully. In your search for knowledge about indoor plants you will find an ally not only in your nurseryman, but also in your neighbour and local newspaper's garden columnist. Glean whatever information you can – the more you know about your plants the more comfortable you'll feel, the greater will be your success and the greener your thumb. Remember, however, that not even the experts win them all; you must be prepared to be wrong now and again and to lose the odd plant. But you'll learn from each mistake and finally develop guidelines resulting in your having a relaxed way with plants.

We hope the information in this book will inspire you with the confidence and enthusiasm to make your indoor garden flourish. Let's go gardening!

Symbols

- Flowering plant
- Foliage plant
- Plant with variegated foliage
- Trailing plant
- Tall plant
- Indigenous plant
- Fruit-bearing plant
- Low-growing plant
- Low-light plant

Useful information

Choosing your plant

Always be open-minded when buying plants. Ask to be shown a range of plants that suit your requirements, remembering that the amount of light it gets is vital, and select from what is offered. There is no point in choosing a plant and then forcing it to adapt to your conditions. If you should see a plant you particularly fancy, then ask if it would suit your requirements. If it doesn't, forget about it.

Should you decide you want the plant anyway, find out as much about it as you can, particularly about a suitable position for it. Then take it home and find the appropriate place in which it will not only survive, but be happy. Never try to force the plant to grow in the wrong position – you won't win!

When buying it is also important to choose the right retail outlet for your purchase. If you know exactly what you need and what conditions will suit the particular plants you buy, then by all means buy from off-the-shelf outlets. But if your knowledge about plants is scant and you need help, then it is far better to go to an accredited member of the South African Nurserymen's Association – be it a nursery or garden centre – where you can obtain advice from a qualified horticulturist.

Look out for the following when buying pot plants:

- The nursery must be clean and tidy. If it is and the plant is well presented, with clean leaves and a clean pot, and if it has a varietal card on it, you at least know that the shopkeeper cares – and that's half the battle won.
- General appearance is most important and even an amateur can recognise whether a plant is looking healthy or not.
- Never buy a tired-looking plant – if it looks that way growing under what should be ideal conditions, imagine what it will look like in the less-than-perfect conditions prevailing in most homes.
- Check foliage for spots and discolourations. Any plant with brown tips or margins is suffering from some form of stress and should be avoided.
- Watch out for limp leaves. These may be due to the plant needing water – an easily corrected problem. If the plant is moist and the leaves limp, then the root system is either not functioning correctly or the plant is suffering from a fungus disease.
- Once you've taken your plant home, study it carefully. See if it needs water, and remove any damaged or dying leaves.

When selecting your plant, always inspect it carefully and buy one in obvious glowing good health. If you have a choice between a big plant which does not look 100 per cent, and a smaller one that is crisp and perky with shiny, clean and glowing leaves, it is generally better to choose the healthier, smaller plant that looks as though it is still growing into its pot. The biggest plant at the lowest price is rarely the right one. If buying a big plant, however, it is often advisable to repot it into a larger pot at the time of purchase, especially if it looks as though it may soon become pot-bound. This will allow it to grow into an even larger specimen, remaining in the new pot without much attention for a number of years.

Should a plant appear to be pot-bound but you want it anyway, ask the horticulturist to replant it for you into a pot just one or two sizes up. You'll have to pay a bit extra for the pot and additional soil but it'll be worth it.

Plants make super gifts, but some people are nervous about handling them. If you are unsure of the gardening capabilities of the person receiving the gift, always ask the sales assistant for a free pamphlet on the care of indoor plants. These are generally available at all nurseries and garden centres registered with the South African Nurserymen's Association.

The success of any plant purchase depends as much on the buyer as the seller – for it is only on the basis of the information you give about your requirements to the horticulturist that he can make recommendations. Your input is vital!

A healthy-looking bromeliad, such as this *Nidularium regelioides* (p. 75), is always a popular choice

The check list below will help you when buying a plant for a specific situation. You will need to give the sales assistant the following details:

- The positioning of your plant. Consider the following:
  a) The light conditions.
  b) Whether the room is airy, draughty or stuffy.
  c) Whether the plant will be placed near a window or door.
- The size and shape of the plant you want; i.e. its height and width.
- If you need foliage, should the leaves be:
  a) Green, coloured or variegated?
  b) Large or small?
  c) Feathery or grassy?
  d) Succulent?
- If you want a flowering plant, is the colour important?

It is most important that you discover how to handle the plant, and whether its care is straightforward or tricky.

You need to know:

- The price of the plant.
- How much light it needs, i.e. where it should be positioned.
- How often it should be watered.
- The room temperature it prefers.
- How much humidity it needs.
- When it will need to be repotted.
- What size pot it will need.
- The correct potting mixture.

The colourful *Primula obconica* (p. 52) is not only pretty, but also an excellent house plant

Plant health

Well-cared for plants are happy plants and are rarely troubled by diseases or pest or insect problems. People are the biggest problem facing house plants – not pests and diseases. It is we humans who put them under stress and weaken them. Indoor plants are generally subjected to either too much kindness or neglect, and the result is the same: plants lose vitality, are vulnerable to attack from all sorts of nasties and often die as a result.

For success with house plants you need to understand your plant and treat it like a child, for like a child its very life depends on you. Plants do not choose to be in homes and offices, in conditions totally alien to them, so it is up to us to care for them by trying to create circumstances as close as possible to those they have in nature.

If you are buying a plant about which you know little or nothing, always check its requirements with the horticulturist selling you the plant. Knowledge will give you confidence, and give your plant not only a good chance of survival, but the opportunity of growing into a lush and healthy plant of which you will be proud and which will give you great joy. The well-cared for plant will hardly ever give any trouble, provided you give it the correct balance of its natural requirements.

Light

On taking your plant into the alien environment of your home, the most important decision is where to place it: near a window with some sun, in bright light but without direct sun, or in a position with little light. Remember, only plastic plants can live in the dark. It is possible to acquire plants for all these positions, but you might find it necessary to move them around a little to find just the right spot. If plants need a little more light than they are getting, you may need to provide artificial light. Plants that are unhappy with the light they are getting will give you problems.

Air circulation

Most plants enjoy good air circulation, without direct draughts, and invariably deteriorate and succumb to pests and diseases when left in hot and stuffy, airless rooms.

Feeding

Generally, it will be unnecessary to fertilise a new plant for about three months. Allow the plant to settle down in its new position before starting its feeding programme.

The basic rules for successful indoor plants:

- Buy a good, healthy plant.
- Place it in the correct position with correct light.
- Water deeply occasionally, rather than a little regularly.
- Avoid overwatering.
- Feed regularly – especially when plants are growing actively – and follow product directions carefully.
- Ensure good air circulation but avoid draughts.
- Keep the leaves clean, sponging off regularly.
- Treat problems promptly.
- Repot when necessary.
- Use correct potting mixtures.
- Remove yellowing and dead leaves regularly.
- Prune when necessary to maintain the plant's shape.

Watering

Watering is different! This you will need to do on a regular basis from the beginning – but do be careful not to overwater. More plants die from overwatering than of any other cause and knowing how much water to give plants is probably the biggest dilemma facing indoor gardeners. The general rule is to water deeply occasionally rather than a little often.

Once waterlogged, roots start to rot and leaf tips turn brown. The invariable reaction of the novice gardener is to think that the plant is drying out and promptly to give it more water, and again more water as it browns some more, confidently believing the poor thing is dying of thirst when in fact the contrary is true. Sadly, the plant eventually dies and the unhappy gardener gives up, convinced that the lack of a green thumb is the problem. Nonsense, it's lack of knowledge!

Unfortunately there are no hard and fast rules about the watering of plants, for the needs of each are different, with some, such as African violets, requiring far more than, say, a succulent or cactus. You will soon get used to individual requirements, but the best way of testing whether a plant needs watering is by poking a finger into the soil to check whether the plant is still moist beneath the surface. You will soon learn that some plants, such as potted azaleas, must never be allowed to dry out, while others, like the lovely trailing cissus, prefer to be almost dry before being watered again. And remember that ferns enjoy a regular light misting with water.

Many busy indoor gardeners who love their plants but have little time to fuss and to test them on a regular daily basis find that a once-a-week watering programme works very well for the majority of indoor plants. However, adjustments must be made for those that do not fit into this regimen, for some may need watering more or less frequently. Also, during spells of exceptionally hot, dry weather, it might be necessary to water more often, while in winter you will probably need to water only every 10 or even 14 days.

Where possible, it is wise to take all your plants outside and to drench them, allowing the water to run right through their pots. Once they have drained properly, take them back indoors and return them to their containers.

Indoor gardeners must always remember that being indoors is an unnatural situation for plants and that they definitely miss the rain. One of the benefits of taking plants outside is that you can gently hose them down, removing any dust and dirt – as rain would in nature. This should be done in the shade to prevent the sun from burning the leaves. Watering in this way also provides an opportunity to examine plants for any blemishes, old leaves which need to be removed, or pest and disease problems.

Drenching the plants outside is also a useful means of washing away unfavourable salts which often build up in the soil of house plants. Municipal water is produced for humans, not plants, and often the salts in it result in a harmful white powdery scum forming on top of the soil, which needs to be washed away. The best water for pot plants is rainwater and it pays to collect roof runoff water in a tank for use on your plant collection. For people in flats, who cannot take their plants outside, it is a good idea to do the same job either at the kitchen sink or in a bath lined with newspapers to prevent the surface from being damaged.

It is very difficult to gauge the amount of water required by plants when they are left standing in containers in their normal positions about the home. People usually either overwater their plants, which results in water gathering in the bottom of saucers and containers, or they water the topsoil, which encourages roots to grow upwards instead of down – a factor which usually adversely affects growth as it results in a shallow root system. It is far better to remove pots from their containers and thoroughly soak them with water. After the excess water has drained away, return them to their original positions. Be careful not to use hot water on plants. This is very dangerous as their fine surface root hairs are extremely sensitive. Tepid water or water at room temperature is the best for your plants. Underwatering of plants is a less frequent problem than overwatering and is normally the result of neglect. Plants talk to us and show their need by wilting, so learn to read the signs. As with our bodies, plants consist of 80 per cent water and simply cannot live without it.

An embodiment of plant health – a well-cared for *Spathiphyllum* 'Mauna Loa' (p. 109)

Humidity and temperature

Humidity and temperature do not cause many problems, but with tropical plants it is wise to create humidity for them during periods of very hot, dry weather. This is done either by misting the leaves occasionally or by placing the pots on humidity trays.

In winter a lack of humidity is often created in rooms by the use of heaters which dry out the air. One of the worst culprits is the fan heater, which should be directed away from plants for it can cause plant scorch. If possible, keep a humidifier in a room with plants.

It is important to keep plants such as cacti and succulents in as dry a position as possible.

Although some plants like higher temperatures than others, you will find that if you can maintain an average indoor temperature of about 22 °C you will have few problems.

Other problems

A few other things to guard against with plants are sunburn and cold-water burn. Many varieties, such as the parlour palm and those other lovely plants for dim places, the aglaonemas, do not like the sun and will burn if left in a bright window, while if you use cold water over some plants' leaves it will also damage them.

Cleaning

To keep plants healthy in our dusty climate it is important to keep leaves clean on both sides – and particularly the undersides, which contain the plant's breathing channels. Washing the leaves' undersides with plain water also reduces the occurrence of red spider. Cleaning is best done by hosing down with a soft spray or by wiping clean with a damp cloth. Special plant wipes are now available. These are ideal, for they are absolutely safe and though non-oily, will still give leaves a shine. In addition they are antistatic which means they will not attract dust. Avoid using any oily substances, such as milk, for cleaning. This will only cause more dust to adhere to the leaves.

Feeding

Modern house plant foods are so effective, yet simple to use, that a great deal of indoor garden maintenance has been done away with. Today, in addition to the regular liquid and granular foods, it is possible to obtain fertilisers in a variety of forms such as powders, which are sprinkled from pepperpot-like dispensers, and spikes and pills which are inserted into the soil. The biggest advantage of most of these modern fertilisers is that they contain slow-release nitrogen which makes them much safer, as it is no longer possible to inflict fertiliser scorch on the roots of plants.

Don't forget to use these fertilisers! Plants, like humans, need a regular balanced diet and this is particularly so when plants are grown in pots. In the garden the roots stretch out further and further in search of food and water, but in a pot they are restricted. As the soil is basically there to keep the plant upright, it becomes necessary for us to supplement the plant's diet with either organic or inorganic foods.

Different plants need different types of foodstuffs, with different quantities of macro- and micro-elements. There are 12 of these essential elements, but basically plants need far more of the macro-elements than the micro-elements. The three macro-elements are nitrogen (N), phosphorus (P) and potassium (K), which are formulated in different ratios to suit different groups of plants.

Among the micro-elements, originally known as trace elements, are molybdenum, zinc, iron, and copper manganese. Of these only a few parts per million are needed; an overdose of micro-elements can cause as much damage as an overdose of the macro-elements.

With the macro-elements, the biggest cause of damage has always been an overdose of nitrogen, but since the development of slow-release (SR) nitrogen formulas this problem has become a thing of the past. Soon these will be the only kinds of fertiliser available.

Depending on whether plants are flowering, fruit-bearing or evergreen, they need different quantities of the elements, hence one sees plant food packets, bottles and fertiliser bags bearing different NPK (nitrogen – phosphorus – potassium ratios).

Although general fertilisers which are suitable for a large variety of plants are available, it is necessary to have some special foods for various groups of plants with specific requirements, such as palms, ferns and African violets. These all need different strengths of the different elements, and although every plant can be catered for, one first needs to know a little about the attributes of the three macro-elements:

Nitrogen (N) provides luxurious, green growth, so is very necessary for plants such as evergreens.

Phosphorus (P) stimulates root growth.

Potassium (K) builds tissue, increases a plant's resistance to diseases and encourages the formation of fruit and flowers.

Depending on the type of plant you have, the most effective combination will be indicated by the formulation of the fertiliser. If this sounds a little complicated, relax. Details printed on bottles and packets explain the purpose of the fertiliser and if you are not sure your local nurseryman or garden centre horticulturist will be able to ensure that you get the right food for the right job.

With the new generation of sophisticated pot plant fertilisers, containing both slow-release nitrogen and some special growth stimulants, it is possible to extend the intervals between applications to as much as two months.

Although all plants must preferably be fed through the soil, they also benefit greatly from being spray-fed through their leaves. This form of fertilising should not be underestimated, as it helps to produce good, lustrous foliage. Foliar foods act rather like tonics for humans. They should be used fortnightly in conjunction with a regular soil-feeding programme.

Remember, never fertilise plants when the soil is very dry – food is best absorbed when the soil is evenly moist. Also, tablet, spike and powder-type fertilisation should be followed by a thorough soaking of the soil in the pot.

The best time for feeding is during spring and summer, when

plants are producing new leaves. And, important though it is to feed plants during their active growth period, it is equally important to give plants a rest during winter. One of the few problems with the slow-release spike or tablet-type fertilisers is that they will go on feeding plants during their rest period, so it is wise, towards the end of summer, to change from slow-release to liquid fertiliser, and to stop fertilising entirely during winter. The only plants that require food throughout the year are those large varieties which are in small pots.

The approach of the semi-dormant or dormant period is indicated in some plants, such as the poinsettia, by the dropping of their leaves, while in others, such as the cyclamen, the leaves die down completely. With evergreens, however, this is not as easy to detect, so be guided by the shortening of the days and cooler weather. The new spring growth is your signal to resume feeding once again.

While all plants need food there are some, such as ferns and African violets, which do not enjoy foliar feeding. Neither do ferns need strong fertilisers. They are best fed with the modern slow-release variety specially prepared for them, or with weak solutions of a general liquid food.

With fertilisers, as with pesticides and insecticides, it is important to use registered products only and to stick to recommended dosages. Too much food will do as much harm as too little. Excessive food may also cause excessive growth, a feature not always welcomed in the home setting where plants of a manageable size are preferable.

In addition to the modern chemical fertilisers, it is also possible to use organic fertilisers. Some of the seaweed and fish extracts are particularly good and ideal for those people who do not believe in using the chemical variety. In the past, these natural forms were very popular because there was less chance of their burning tender roots, a problem inherent in the older types of chemical fertilisers. The development of slow-release nitrogen has, however, solved this problem.

Whether you use chemical or organic fertilisers, it is important that you feed your plants. Remember, they rely on you!

Repotting

All pot plants must be repotted from time to time. Repotting should only be done when necessary and usually a plant will let you know when the time has come – either by losing condition or by pushing its roots through the drainage holes. Generally, it is unnecessary to repot plants that are looking healthy and are continuing to produce healthy new leaves.

Should you feel it necessary to check on the condition of a plant's roots, this is done fairly easily with plants in smaller pots. Soak the plant and pot thoroughly. Then, with the palm of your hand placed over the surface of the soil and the stem between your fingers, invert the pot and tap it sharply. The whole root ball should slide out. If this does not work, it might be necessary to slide a knife blade around the rim of the pot, as occasionally the roots become firmly attached to the sides of the pot.

An assortment of implements and materials required for repotting

Repotting
1 Time to repot 2 Remove plant from pot 3 Gently separate roots 4 Add crock and layer of river sand 5 Position plant 6 Fill in with potting soil

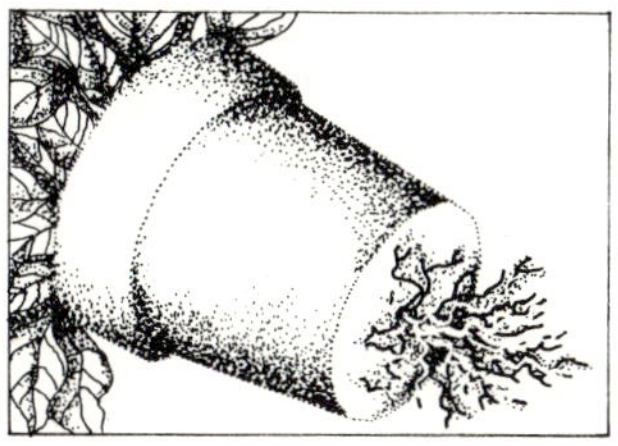
1

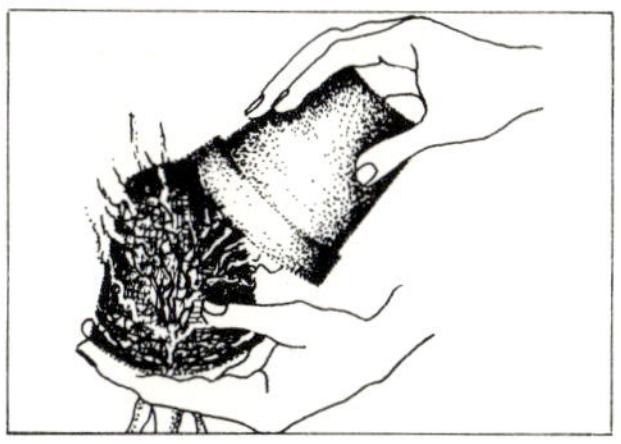
2

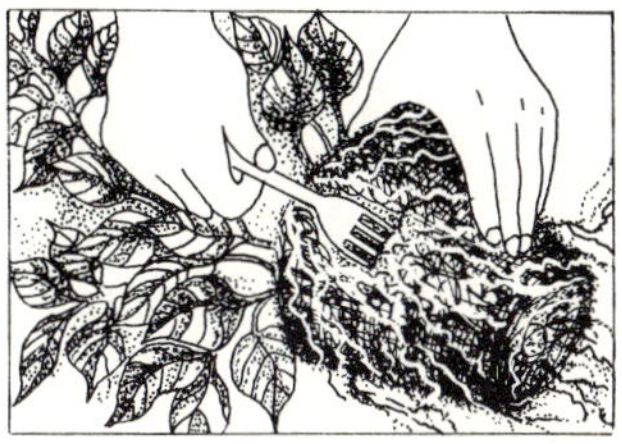
3

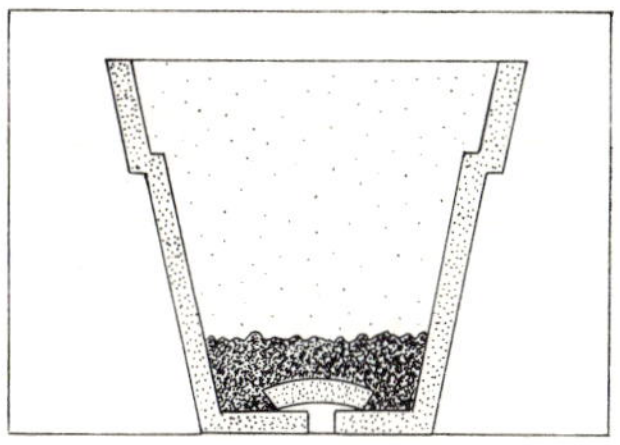
4

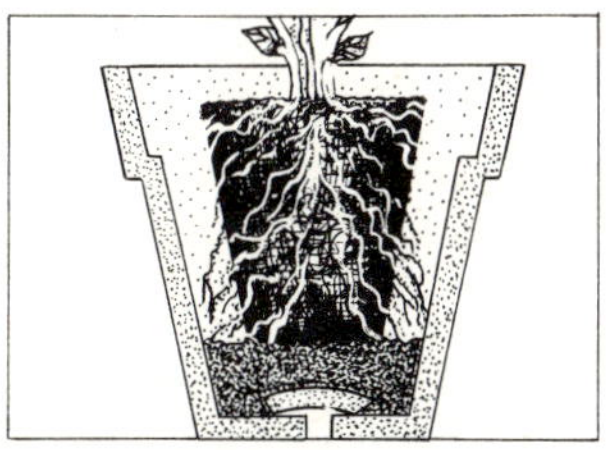
5

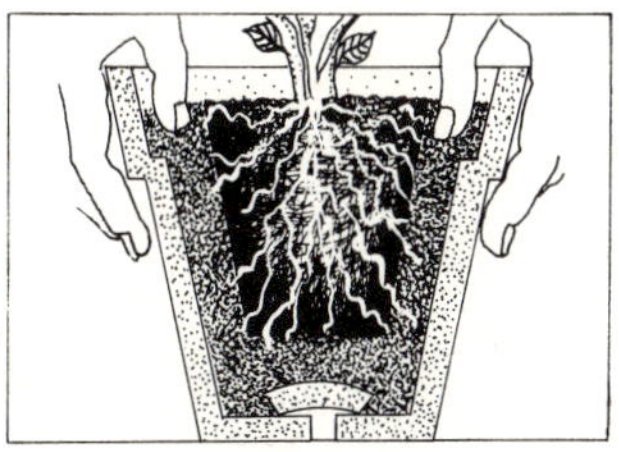
6

Times to repot

If there are only a few roots in evidence around the sides of the root ball, apologise to your plant and gently return it to its original position. The time to repot is when the root ball shows a good but not crowded cover of roots over the entire soil surface, with some soil still showing.

If the root ball is a mass of tightly twisted roots, with no soil showing, then it is definitely time to repot and it may be necessary to separate the roots gently and perhaps even root prune them to encourage fresh growth. If the roots are very crowded it is a good idea to take a sharp blade and make shallow cuts from the top to the bottom of the root frame, every 8 cm or so around the circumference of the root ball, so that it's easier to separate the roots before repotting. Also try to remove any crocks or pebbles which may be attached to the roots at the base of the root ball. Remove any old soil left on the surface or at the base, later replacing it with fresh potting soil.

Root pruning

When root pruning, it is also necessary to trim some of the growth above ground, so that the reduced root system does not have to support an excessive number of leaves.

Repotting preparations

Before starting your repotting programme, it is important to have all the necessary materials and implements as well as your new pots ready for the operation (see the check list on p. 16). Generally, each plant needs to be moved up one pot size larger than before. Indoor plants should be kept rather snug in their pots, for if there is too much soil around them the excess soil does not dry out properly, and this has an adverse effect on the plant.

If you are using terracotta pots, these are best left soaking in water for a couple of hours before use, so that the dry clay can absorb sufficient water instead of soaking up all the water in the soil which was actually meant for the plant.

Potting soil

When repotting, the growing medium is vital. It is unwise to use soil from your garden. This may carry pathogens or diseases and will certainly not have the correct texture. When taken out of a garden environment, ordinary soil quickly compacts and loses its ability to hold moisture or provide quick drainage.

Roots need oxygen and plants will either grow poorly or die if the soil is so compacted that the tiny air spaces in the medium remain waterlogged. Rather use a commercial potting soil. Soils specially blended are light and airy, drain well and allow for easy root growth. They have the right ratio of big and small particles to retain moisture, yet allow the draining of excess water.

Commercial potting soils are an ideal growing medium for the majority of house plants, but for some, such as African

Repotting a cactus
1 Wearing gloves, slide out cactus 2 Place crock over drainage hole 3 Holding cactus by newspaper wrapped around it, replace on layer of river sand 4 Fill in with soil and top with layer of pebbles

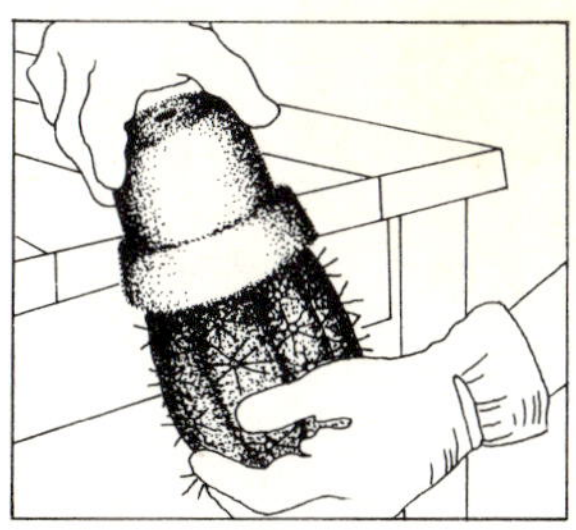
1

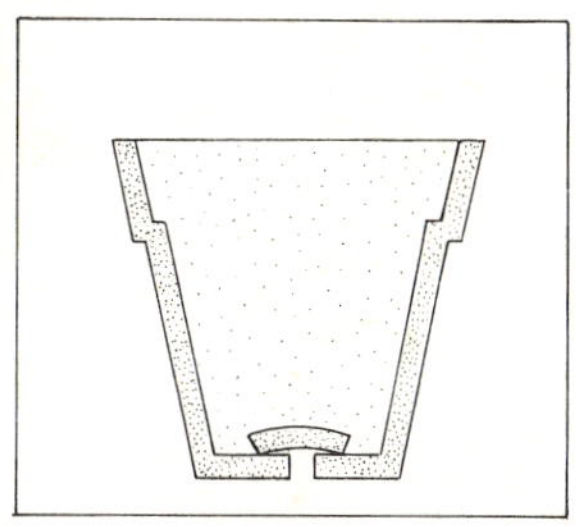
2

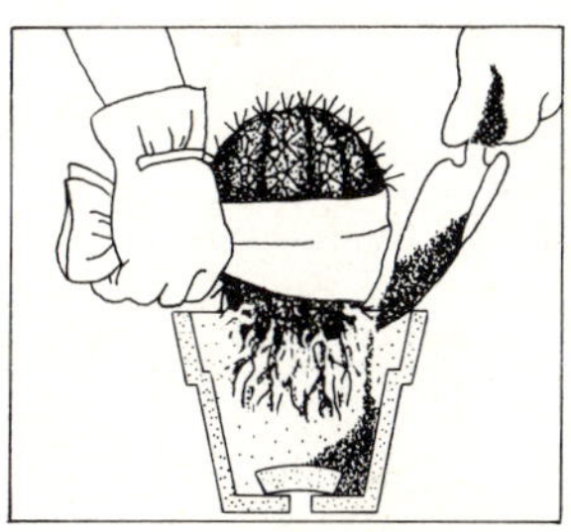
3

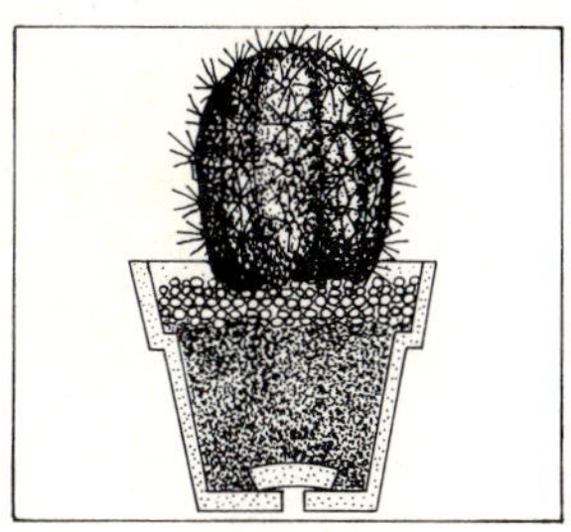
4

The following is a good potting soil mixture (use a bucket as a measure): two parts unsifted compost; three parts good garden loam; two parts coarse river sand; a half-part well-rotted old kraal manure, and a heaped cupful of either bone meal or superphosphate. Should you require the soil to be slightly acid, include half a bucket of dampened imported peat moss or acid compost. This also helps to retain moisture.

violets, ferns and cymbidium orchids, specialist soils are available from your local garden centre. Commercial soils are sterilised, weed-free and blended in the correct ratios. They save the gardener a tremendous amount of time and trouble, and improve the chances of success. There is also no occurrence of the diseases often associated with home blends.

For the enthusiast who wishes to do everything himself, the best formula for a potting medium is: a rich garden loam; organic material such as well-rotted leaf mould, compost or peat moss; a slow-acting organic fertiliser such as kraal manure or bone meal; and a gritty soil lightener such as washed coarse river sand or vermiculite or perlite. When blending, the aim should be for a rich but light and friable mixture that retains moisture, yet is sufficiently porous to drain water easily.

Drainage
Drainage is the most important factor in the life of any pot plant, for without it the soil remains soggy and causes root rot. Always choose pots with one or more holes in the base. Cover the base with a piece of wire gauze, broken crocks, pebbles, coarse river sand or even coir through which the water can easily drain without your soil washing away.

Once this is done, place a shallow layer of coarse river sand above the drainage material and then centre the present pot on top of this layer of soil. Fill the area around it with more soil, leaving an exact hollow into which to drop your plant. Otherwise, merely place the plant on top of the soil and slowly work in some soil, gently pressing it firmly around the roots as you go. Always ensure that the stem of the plant is in the centre of the pot and do not fill above the original soil line, which should be about 2,5 cm below the rim of the pot, to allow sufficient space for proper watering.

Once repotted, saturate the plant with water but do not fertilise for at least a month to give the plant a chance to settle into its new pot and start growing actively. Then start to feed with a recommended liquid fertiliser.

Check list of implements and materials required for repotting:

• A selection of pots in various sizes.

• One of the following materials to cover drainage holes to prevent loss of soil while ensuring that excess water can escape: crocks (broken pieces of terracotta), wire gauze or coir.

• River sand or pebbles.

• Potting soils of various kinds – general or specialist, depending on your task.

• A good pair of secateurs for trimming away decaying matter, damaged sections of the plant and for root pruning.

• A scoop for lifting soil.

• A small watering can.

• Rubber gloves.

The right pot

Pots and containers are important to indoor plants for a variety of reasons. They can be decorative or functional, or add something to a plant's personality. And from a practical point of view they are, of course, vital.

In nature plant roots wander where they may, but indoors they are confined and as a result the pots in which they are grown are all-important to their future development. For practical purposes flower pots come in a range of sizes from 5-35 cm (top width or diameter and depth are the same). The pot should match the size of the plant's root system. For instance an African violet is normally grown in a 9 cm pot. To plant it in a smaller pot would not only crowd its roots but would result in the need for more frequent watering and feeding. Overpotting, on the other hand, often results in root rot – the soil remains moist for too long a period as the plant is unable to absorb all the moisture quickly enough.

Choosing the right pot size
There are no hard and fast rules about the size of a pot in relation to a plant, but a successful rule of thumb is for a pot to be approximately a third of the total height of the pot and plant.

In addition to the timeless flower pot there are of course many other types of large and small containers. The two most frequently found in good garden shops are the azalea-shape, with a depth three-quarters that of its width, and the bowl, with a depth half that of its width. The azalea pot is generally used for azaleas, as its name implies, but also for plants such as calceolarias and chrysanthemums and for groups of small plants. The bowl is preferred for low-growing varieties such as peace-in-the-home, cacti and particularly for bulbs, such as hyacinths and daffodils. Often the choice of pots is merely a matter of taste, but one practical consideration is that a tall plant in a light soil mixture is less likely to topple over in a broader pot than in a taller one.

When a plant outgrows its pot – this is usually indicated by the roots either starting to push their way through the drainage holes at the base of the pot or by lifting the soil at the top – it is wise to repot it into a new pot one or two sizes larger, depending on the plant's growth rate. Many people think that by putting a plant into a much larger pot it will grow faster or that they'll have to repot it less frequently. It doesn't work that way, however, and your plant will also look awkward and out of proportion.

Often if a plant has reached the optimum size suited to its position it may be maintained in its underpotted state by pruning and root pruning it to keep it healthy. It will be necessary to water and feed it more regularly and to supplement its diet to replenish the nutrients in the depleted soil medium.

Containers are available in a variety of shapes, sizes and materials

Choosing the right pot

A major controversy concerning the choice of practical growing pots has for many years been whether to use terracotta or plastic pots. Economics has now made such arguments irrelevant, for today the price of terracotta has virtually precluded it as a contender, except for decorative purposes.

Growers today use plastic pots, not only because of the price but also because they are lighter, less bulky and easier to stack. They also retain moisture better than their more attractive terracotta counterparts. With the correct potting mixture, plastic pots should drain equally well as terracotta and should also adequately retain moisture. Those who can afford them often prefer the old-fashioned terracotta pots which are almost as old as man himself. They do have certain advantages. Aesthetics is, of course, an important consideration if you are not using a decorative pot cover, and due to their weight, the plants are more stable. Because the clay is porous, it breathes, allowing oxygen to reach the soil from all directions and so encourages root development.

The porous nature of terracotta pots does, however, have certain disadvantages. Firstly, the soil becomes drier far more quickly than in their plastic counterpart. This is, in fact, an advantage for such plants as cacti and our many indigenous succulents, which appreciate drier conditions than the average plant.

One of the disadvantages of porous terracotta pots is that ugly salt deposits as well as fungus, moss and mould often form on their sides. Sometimes, however, this adds to the decorative charm and character of the pots and can look very pleasing.

Despite all the arguments for and against terracotta or plastic pots, the plants themselves are really happy to grow in virtually anything from tin cans to yoghurt cups. The choice of a decorative container is much more a matter of individual preference, and requires some careful thought.

Decorative containers

There is no doubt that certain plants look better in certain styles of containers, depending on their shape, colour and character. Green plants, for example, look stunning in brass, while flowering plants such as chrysanthemums and African violets look best in colourful glazed plain or fancy pots, or in different kinds of baskets, while cane undoubtedly suits the palm court look.

Size also plays an important role in the choice of containers and large, locally made glazed pot holders are now readily available for big plants such as ficuses, scheffleras and palms. Wooden, bamboo or cane boxes in the style of Versailles planters look very good in entrances, large living rooms, studios and studies, patios and sun rooms.

There was a time when plastic containers were looked down on and considered not quite proper, but today there are many very attractive modular styles available which are particularly well suited to offices. Easy to clean and often with built-in caster-style wheels for ease of movement, they are generally designed in such a way that the pot plant cannot stand in the water which gathers at the base as a result of overwatering. If such an aid is not provided it is a good idea to fill the bottom of your container with pebbles on which to rest your flower pot so that it can't touch any water that collects.

Overwatering is always a problem with indoor plants. It is important to choose pot covers that are not porous to prevent water rings from marking tables, wooden floors and carpets. Baskets, for example, should be sufficiently large to accommodate a plastic drip tray as well as the pot.

Fortunately manufacturers today usually design all kinds of pot covers in brass, copper, ceramic or basketware to fit the standard size plastic growing pots. If you find there is insufficient room for a saucer in the bottom of the pot cover, line it with a sheet of plastic or heavy-duty tinfoil.

Many attractive ceramic pots with trays are available for growing your plants indoors, but generally it is better to place your plant in its plastic pot into a container. This not only prevents water spillage or seepage but looks neater and more attractive.

Avoid planting directly into a container or pot of any kind without drainage holes, as it makes it difficult to control the amount of moisture needed by the plant. Invariably the plant has to grow in a soggy soil mixture, which causes root rot and eventual death. Growing plants in containers without drainage holes requires exceptional care.

Decorative containers are available in a huge range of materials, shapes and sizes. The materials include clear glass, ceramic, brass, plastic, fibre cement and fibreglass in either very simple or very ornate designs. The choice is vast, but always remember that it is the plant you want to show off to its best advantage, not the pot. So be very careful to choose a container that is attractive but discreet, and that will enhance the plant's character rather than diminish it. It must, of course, also complement the rest of your décor. Basketware, for example, looks totally out of place in a formally furnished room, while brass is far too grand for a sun room and plastic generally seems better suited to offices and the world of commerce.

Today one also finds a wide range of containers for hanging plants, but always be careful where you hang these or you might have water spilling on furniture and carpets. Although many come with built-in saucers, the water often fills and spills from the saucer if you are not careful. Many decorative chains are available from hardware stores and can be used to hang all sorts of containers at different levels.

Plant arrangements

Plants today are as much a part of interior decorating as furniture, lighting, paintings and curtaining and are used everywhere in the home. Look at any glossy magazine and you'll find them not only in the entertainment and play rooms but also in the bedroom, kitchen, bathroom and other smaller rooms.

Potted plants are no longer merely beautiful objects. They do more than decorate; they impart atmosphere and serve many valuable purposes in interior landscape, from indicating direction and acting as screens and room dividers, to creating focal points. Plants provide not only colour and texture but cool hot rooms and give life to dull ones.

The plant has come a long way since Victorian times when just a few - such as the sword fern, sentry palm and mother-in-law's tongue - were used singly in bay windows and dreary hallways. For many years after that - until well after World War II - one could have been forgiven for thinking that the rubber plant was the only indoor plant in the world.

Today there is a new sophistication. Plants are not merely dotted about but form part of our overall decorating schemes, with specimen plants providing the same decorative impact as stylish furniture or even sculptures.

Although decorating with plants, like any other form of decorating, is a very personal matter, there are several guidelines the home decorator should follow in order to avoid disaster, for plants, unlike other objets d'art in the home, are not inanimate but living, growing, vital entities.

Though it may sound trite, the home owner must first of all be prepared to look after the plants, for they cannot look after themselves. Secondly, their living conditions must be considered and it might be necessary to check these with a horticulturist at your local nursery.

Some items of importance which must be taken into consideration when acquiring new plants are:

Surroundings: One must be careful not to place multi-leafed plants, such as ferns, or those with variegated foliage, against busy wallpapers, nor plants with coloured leaves against matching backgrounds. On the other hand, a very bold-leafed plant such as a birdsnest fern will look superb against a stark wall, and a plant with a tracery of light leaves will show up well against a dark wall. Plants generally look best in uncluttered rooms, although collections of small plants can often be very effective in cottagey surroundings.

Colour: This is a tricky subject where restraint must be the keynote. Colour, whether it be foliage or flowers, is best used to highlight a group of plants, lighten an arrangement which has little contrast or to enhance a situation. For example, the new golden sword fern 'Boston Gold', with its striking shape and strong, beautiful yellowy-green leaves, will lift a group of green ferns. Colour must always be considered very carefully in relation to the overall scheme. Play colour down rather than make a feature of it, particularly in a room which already has strong colour impact.

There are three main foliage colours among indoor plants: green, yellow and red or pink, but look out for and make use of the occasional greys and blues that some of the bromeliads and aglaonemas among others offer.

There's a great choice of greens, from light green through to almost black green, in both large and small plants. Many plants with variegated leaves, such as crotons, which often blend all three colours in one leaf, and variegated scheffleras, dieffenbachias and peperomias, have brighter hues. The reds and pinks are found in such plants as begonias, dracaenas and cordylines, while the lovely and useful small pink plant commonly known as the polka-dot plant blends beautifully at the front of arrangements and looks great in single-variety groups on coffee and side tables. Another colourful low-growing plant is the *Maranta leuconeura erythroneura*, with its striking cerise-veined leaves.

Bromeliads were mentioned earlier, and mixed in groupings, they can provide a stunning show on their own. There are many different kinds, and by blending them with moss and driftwood it is possible to produce a landscaped scene in your home. Many of them have bright centres, leaves of startling greens, and produce weird and exotically beautiful spikes of flowers. Although they do well inland, they are an absolute must for humid coastal conditions, particularly in subtropical Natal.

Shapes: Bold plants such as the large-leafed *Ficus* varieties, beaucarneas (such as the elephant's foot plant) and striking palms are very dramatic in modern surroundings with modern furniture, but a total disaster in a country cottage, where the less harsh lines of plants such as the trailing cissus, marantas,

Right: Plant arrangements can be used successfully in the decorating of a room

wandering Jew (*Tradescantia* varieties) and little button ferns prove more suitable.

Scale: Plants must neither swamp their surroundings nor be overwhelmed by them. Thus in the large modern studio with big blank walls and huge expanses of glass, tiddly little African violets, fittonias and the like are totally lost. What is needed is something that can make a statement, such as a large *Ficus benjamina* or any of the other big members of the ficus genus, like a large-leafed fiddle-leaf fig or an old fashioned rubber plant, which is still a very valuable decorating prop.

Space: Do not jam plants together. Give them breathing space so that their leaves can unfurl and spread naturally and new growth is not distorted. Crowded conditions not only spoil the effect of the plant, but also spoil the shape of the plant and result in the yellowing of leaves. Crowding may even encourage pests - plants enjoy a bit of air.

Containers: The choice of a plant container is most important and is discussed fully in a separate chapter but remember that pots should complement and not detract from plants. Similar-style containers, such as clay or single-colour pots, should be grouped together. A hotchpotch of different colours and styles can be very distracting. A single-patterned container, provided the design is not too bold, can be attractive for displaying a specimen plant, but a clutch of patterned pots can look horrendous. It is safer to stick to the old faithfuls, such as baskets and white or single-colour pots, which blend in with most objects.

Groupings: Try obtaining a three-dimensional effect by mixing shapes, thereby giving a sense of space and variety. You can add depth by positioning a conspicuous plant either in front or to the side of the others.

Neatness: Plants must be kept tidy, washed and dusted. Take them outside and rinse them down occasionally, sponging their leaves at the same time to remove the dirt - there is nothing drearier than dusty, tired-looking plants. Old flowers and leaves must be removed and slightly damaged ones trimmed with scissors. Surfaces, too, must be kept clean and it pays to move all the plants from their normal positions for a good cleaning at least once a week. Also wash off water marks and remove any leaf litter decomposing in saucers and containers.

Contrasting leaf colours add interest to plant arrangements

Expense: It is amazing how often people complain about the price of plants and then promptly pay thousands of rands for a painting or piece of sculpture to achieve an effect which a plant could have achieved equally well or better at a fraction of the cost. Some big and bold plants may well cost a fair amount of money, but then they provide the decorative punch normally provided by large pieces of furniture.

Positioning

Plants may be used practically anywhere in the home, but there are certain places that simply cry out for them and where they are extremely effective, adding life to dead spots, colour to bleak backgrounds and softness to areas that need screening.

Kitchens: In a rather sterile-looking kitchen, particularly if there is a handy deep windowsill, it is possible to make very attractive displays. Kitchens, which are generally on the south side of homes in South Africa, have gentle but bright light that suits many plants very well. Try to create a theme by blending either colours or styles of plants, for some plants form a natural unity.

Cupboard facings in kitchens can be softened very successfully by placing an attractive trailing plant such as a cissus to hang down over a door which is rarely opened. Blended with copper pots and the normal kitchen knick-knacks, such as jelly moulds and brown ceramic hens filled with eggs, dark green plants turn a kitchen into one of the most exciting rooms in the house - particularly if you use some of the super new hi-tech coloured plastic containers to blend with kitchen cupboards, appliances and finishes.

Be careful not to clutter work tops. Rather find a handy, out-of-the-way corner which will take a plant, or place plants on the surrounds of a breakfast bar counter, table or dining nook. Hanging plants may also be used successfully in kitchens, but take care not to cut out light from working surfaces.

Bathrooms: Bathrooms, particularly very light ones, can be excellent plant centres, and plants certainly help soften the clinical surroundings. The humidity produced by hot baths and showers, often several times a day, suits many plants admirably, particularly many of the tropical plants which are accustomed to steamy conditions.

Shelf-space is often at a premium in bathrooms, but cupboard tops are handy, particularly for trailing varieties. Air plants take up little space and enjoy the occasional burst of moist air. Where space is not a problem some of the palms such as the sentry palm and the parlour palm do well, as do the large-leafed birdsnest fern and both the large and small spathiphyllums. An excellent trailer for bathrooms is the indigenous hen and chicks. Provided there is sufficient light, small bowls of African violets help to brighten basin-side shelves and dressing table tops.

Stairwells: Another place where plants are often needed is at the base of a stairwell. The light is rarely good in such places and so a combination of plants capable of taking low light, such as most of the dracaenas and the aglaonemas, would be successful. If there is just a little bit of light you might add a peace lily, that lovely leafy spathiphyllum, with its beautiful white flag-like spathes and deep-green foliage.

Bay windows: The old-fashioned bay window is a wonderful position for plants, and there one can really go to town, with some plants hanging from the ceiling and a variety of others of differing heights ranged around, using the window as a picture frame in which you design your landscape. Remember that sky is as important as the plants - don't overcrowd it!

Problem areas: A narrow wall, such as that between a window and door, can often be a problem. A piece of furniture placed in front of it usually looks awkward or cramped, but a plant can be used to unite the areas on either side. A group of plants at different levels, perhaps even placed on wooden, perspex or metal cubes, can be turned into a feature.

If you are faced with areas such as narrow windowsills or shelves, try placing a few plants forward and a few as far back as possible. Also try varying the heights.

Be bold and creative

While plants may be used as furniture to screen or separate, don't let them become part of the furniture by leaving them in exactly the same spot year after year. Be bold and creative and move them about. Try new combinations and don't be foolish enough to hold on to a half-dead plant that you think might recover. Throw it out and get a new one. If you have confidence in it then rather take it outside and allow it to recuperate under a tree, returning it when it's looking presentable once again.

It's important to group together plants that enjoy similar conditions, particularly if they're to be planted together in one container. If you plant a cactus, which has a low water requirement, with a moisture-loving button fern, for example, you're asking for problems. Nor is it any good mixing a fern that enjoys bright light with low-light plants in a dim position.

Before buying plants, try to read up a bit about them, then check with the horticulturist where to place them and what their watering and humidity requirements are.

Once you see how plants can make a room come to life, you'll wonder how you ever lived without them. Plants are fun, and mixing them together to create indoor landscapes can become a fascinating hobby. Enjoy it!

Office plantscapes

Plants have become vital to modern office environments, providing a touch of serene nature in the alien environment of glass, concrete and steel. Interior plantscapes play many roles apart from being purely decorative, providing both those who work in the building and those who visit it with a feeling of peace and tranquillity, even a sense of wellbeing. This calming influence has resulted in greater productivity and impresses potential clients and customers.

From a purely practical point of view plants make excellent screens, creating a sense of privacy. They also form natural barriers, absorb noise and informally determine traffic flow.

It is important that someone should look after plants in the office to keep them green and attractive. Plants are not designed to survive the rigours of such a foreign environment and nothing looks worse than tired and dreary pot plants. Fortunately, certainly for the more affluent concerns, there are professional plantscapers. They provide design and consultancy services with regard to plants and containers as well as the technicalities of lighting, feeding and watering, and also offer a guaranteed maintenance service.

Atriums are the latest trend in today's modern office blocks and the professionals are certainly needed here. They should be called in at the drawing board stage to work with and advise architects, landscape architects and interior designers on how to create the correct environment for plants, so avoiding costly mistakes and unnecessary additional expenses later.

The secretary or receptionist faced with the task of decorating office and waiting room areas with plants should seek the advice of a reputable plant dealer at either a nursery or garden centre.

Horticulturists should be given as much information as possible about the function for which the plants are required. They also need to know whether tall, low-growing or table top plants are required and under what conditions and in what positions they will be required to live. Factors such as light, air movement and air-conditioning are vital.

Fortunately there are many plants that grow very well indoors - even with air-conditioning. In fact, many plants thrive in well-regulated, air-conditioned areas with their even temperatures and set humidity levels.

Light, or rather the lack of it, is probably the single biggest problem facing office plants, but if they are well chosen for the conditions, with the assistance of some good artificial light it is possible to maintain beautiful indoor gardens with a minimum of effort. The worst possible way to test light is using only your eyes - it is worth investing in a simple light meter. These are inexpensive and well worth the money, for they invariably pay for themselves over and over again by enabling you to maintain plants successfully rather than having to keep on buying new ones only to have them also deteriorate and die.

According to IPSA, the Interior Plantscapers' Association, who have provided much of the information for this chapter, the ideal light for most plants is 750 lux and the absolute minimum 500 lux. In most offices in South Africa, certainly in the old-fashioned ones, it is rarely much more than 250 lux.

Where lighting is poor and natural light cannot be improved, supplementary artificial lighting proves very successful. The cool-white fluorescent lamps are the best - particularly in reasonably low-ceilinged areas. They show true plant colours and are the standard by which other lamps are measured. In areas with high ceilings, such as atriums, lobbies and stores, high intensity discharge (HID) lamps are more efficient for plant maintenance.

Where no natural light is available, artificial light may be used successfully as the sole light source. It may even serve a dual role: that of room lighting and plant lighting. General room lighting may need to be supplemented in the vicinity of the plant to solve any problems.

Plants can be of vital importance in office surroundings

Few problems should be encountered by plants in normal offices where reasonable light and a fairly regular temperature is maintained 365 days of the year. But they do suffer stress in many of the older buildings where lights and air-conditioning systems are turned off over weekends and often for as long as a fortnight over Christmas. In winter the plants, particularly those on the outer edges of buildings, suffer from the sharp drop in temperature, while in summer the rooms suddenly become hot and stuffy.

Watering is another important factor in the life of office plants. This needs to be carefully regulated, for generally the less light a plant has, the less water it needs. While most plants should be checked once a week, it may not be necessary to water them that often. One of the most successful ways of checking to see whether a plant needs watering is to use one of the modern moisture meters, which are often combined with light meters. The most effective method, however, is to use the thumb or finger test. To avoid messing up manicured nails, insert a matchstick or frozen-ice stick into the soil. If this is damp when withdrawn, no water is needed.

More plants are killed by kindness than neglect, so gardeners must be careful not to overwater. Also, regularly remove pots from their holders to ensure that no water has collected at the bottom. This invariably causes roots to rot and plants to die.

Plantscapers in South Africa are today using a new pot system. It is a hybrid version of hydroculture – the method of growing plants in water – and the normal soil culture method. Normal plastic flower pots that have not had holes punched into their bases are used.

A plastic tube, slightly taller than the pot, is placed against the inside wall of the pot. About a third of the pot is then filled with leca clay pellets. To ease the flow of water through the pipe

PLANTS FOR OFFICES

The following plants have been tried and tested by interior plantscapers and have proved extremely suitable for office and home interiors:

Plants for air-conditioned offices
Aglaonema varieties
Anthurium varieties
Arecastrum romanzoffianum
Aspidistra elatior
Beaucarnea recurvata
Calathea varieties
Chamaedorea elegans
Chamaedorea seifritzii
Chrysalidocarpus lutescens
Cissus rhombifolia
Codiaeum varieties
Cordyline fruticosa varieties
Dizygotheca elegantissima
Dracaena varieties
Fatsia japonica
Ficus varieties
Howea varieties
Maranta varieties
Monstera deliciosa
Philodendron varieties
Phoenix roebelenii
Rhapis excelsa
Sansevieria varieties
Schefflera actinophylla
Schefflera arboricola
Scindapsus aureus
Spathiphyllum varieties
Syngonium varieties
Yucca elephantipes

Plants for poor light conditions
Adiantum varieties
Aglaonema varieties
Aspidistra elatior
Bromeliad varieties
Chamaedorea elegans
Chamaedorea seifritzii
Dracaena varieties
Howea varieties
Philodendron varieties
Sansevieria varieties
Spathiphyllum varieties
Syngonium podophyllum 'White Butterfly'

Flowering varieties (temporary spot accent)
Anthurium varieties
Azalea varieties
Bromeliad varieties
Chrysanthemum varieties
Coleus varieties (colourful leaves)
Cymbidium hybrids
Euphorbia pulcherrima
Kalanchoe blossfeldiana
Saintpaulia ionantha varieties
Spathiphyllum varieties

Desktop plants
Aglaonema varieties
Azalea varieties
Calathea varieties
Chamaedorea elegans
Chrysanthemum hybrids
Euphorbia pulcherrima
Kalanchoe blossfeldiana
Maranta varieties
Nephrolepis exaltata 'Tuffii'
Philodendron varieties (small kinds)
Saintpaulia ionantha varieties
Scindapsus aureus
Spathiphyllum wallisii
Syngonium podophyllum 'White Butterfly'

Plants for good light conditions
Adiantum varieties
Codiaeum varieties
Euphorbia pulcherrima
Hedera helix varieties
Kalanchoe blossfeldiana
Phoenix roebelenii
Schefflera arboricola
Yucca elephantipes

into the pot, it is useful to make a small nick in the lower edge of the pipe; otherwise it may sit flush on the bottom of the pot and prevent the water from flowing properly. Place a soil separator made of Bidim, a felt-like substance, on top of the leca. The normal potting soil in which the plant will grow is added on top of this. Once the plant has been potted, water is poured down the pipe to fill the leca 'tank'. The level of this water may be maintained either by using a stick or a pipette.

With this method the plant takes up as much water as it needs. The water from the 'tank' is drawn up from the leca clay pebbles, through the separator and into the soil by means of capillary action. Plantscapers have found that this system is both simple and easy to maintain and that it reduces maintenance to about once every three weeks, for the plants do not need to be watered as regularly. An added advantage is that the plant may easily be given liquid or powder food via the pipe, and with some of the slow-release hydroponic foods available the frequency of this job is also considerably reduced.

Buildings are designed for the comfort of humans rather than plants, but fortunately plants are reasonably happy with both the temperature and humidity levels set for humans. Most interior plants prefer a day temperature of 21-24° C, which is just a little higher than human beings' preference.

In most buildings the humidity level is maintained between 50 and 55 per cent, although it may fall to as low as 20 per cent. Though many plants, particularly those from the tropical rain forests which form the greater majority of successful indoor plants, enjoy a relatively high humidity and may take up to 85 per cent humidity, they are generally happy to tolerate humidities as low as 40 per cent. Fortunately humans feel discomfort below this level and under such circumstances humidifiers are usually installed, which in turn assist the plants.

The modern air-conditioned office should have no dust, but it is surprising how plants that are left untended become dirty. Dust blocks the pores which regulate the plants' 'breathing', while it also reduces the light reaching them, so it is important to keep plants clean. This is best done by using the special wipes now available, as they contain natural oils which do not harm the plant. Use the aerosol leafshine sprays only when absolutely necessary, as some of them have a high oil content which may harm the plants. A soft cloth with plain water which includes just a few drops of dish-washing liquid may also be used. This type of treatment is best suited to plants with hard, waxy type leaves, while those with hairy or soft leaves are best cleaned by using a soft watercolour paintbrush or washing them under the tap in the early part of the day. Leave them all day to dry out again – this reduces the possibility of fungus disease.

There are exceptions to every rule and learning to live with plants can be very much a matter of trial and error. However, anyone who buys quality plants and who follows the general principles discussed above should have few problems. If problems do crop up, the horticulturist at the local nursery is only a phone call away.

Pests and problems

If, despite taking proper care of your plants, you still have pests and problems, then you will have to resort to using the correct fungicide or insecticide. When doing this always ensure that you use a registered product, taking the advice of your local plant doctor, nurseryman or horticulturist at your favourite nursery. Official registration means that if the product is used according to the instructions, it will not only provide proper control but will not damage plants or be hazardous to the health of humans or animals. Without these qualities it would not be registered, but do remember the key phrase is 'use according to instructions'.

The correct application of any treatment is vital, for the best product in the world will not be effective and may even cause damage if used incorrectly. In mixing, use exact quantities, for twice as much is not twice as effective – you can only kill any insect or pest once. What's more, it would be a total waste of money.

Although there are many insects in the world, experts tell us that less than one per cent of them are considered pests. There are two methods to control them, depending on how the insects feed. These are the use of either 'contact' or 'systemic' insecticides. The first kills on contact or as a result of sprayed foliage being eaten by such insects as beetles and caterpillars. With the latter method the insecticide is absorbed by the plant and is particularly effective for the control of sucking insects such as aphids.

Fungicides are for fungus problems such as mildew, black spot and rust. These are most often used as preventative measures, for the problems crop up in cool, damp and humid conditions and are not always easy to identify before harm is done. Regular spray programmes should be set up for plants prone to attack, such as roses.

Fortunately the days of having to mix insecticides for indoor plants are gone. Today special, easy-to-use, wide-spectrum aerosol sprays are available to control both insects and fungus pests. The joy of these sprays is that as soon as a pest is discovered it can be treated promptly, before it has time to spread. Remember, when using any insecticide, spray both on top and underneath leaves.

Plant pins are also useful for the protection of indoor plants. These are pushed into the soil and are effective for many weeks. During watering, the systemic insecticide with which the pins are impregnated is taken up by the roots and distributed to all parts of the plant.

These pins are particularly useful for ferns, for few ferns will tolerate pesticides, or for that matter even fertiliser, on their leaves. They are best treated with pesticides, as well as fed, at the roots.

Fortunately there are not many insects and pests which bother indoor plants. They are limited to sucking insects, a few chewing varieties, and some fungal diseases.

Although ants are often seen on pot plants they are not really a problem, but instead prove useful in attracting one's attention to a problem. On close inspection of your plant you will discover that it either has aphids or scale insects, which attract the ants. Once you rid the plants of these pests the ants will disappear like magic – it's the insects they're after, not your plants.

Use the following table to identify and control pests and diseases.

American bollworm

Scale insects

Looper worm

PESTS	DAMAGE	CONTROL
American bollworm Hairy caterpillars, varying in colour from light to dark green with a prominent stripe on either side of their bodies. Vary in length from 10-20 mm. Feet closely interspersed over the entire length of their bodies. Found on any green material, fruit or leaves.	Chew away sides of leaves and buds.	A variety of systemic and contact garden sprays.
Aphids Small, 1-2 mm long, pear-shaped black or green insects. Always found in colonies on the young growth of plants.	Because they are sap-sucking insects, aphids cause leaves to wilt and curl, retarding growth.	A variety of both systemic and contact, aphicide sprays are available as well as plant pins for insertion in the soil.
Looper worm Light green with sparse hair and rather shiny body. Has legs in front and at the back of its body causing it to loop its body, undulating as it moves.	Chews away sides of leaves and new buds. Also attacks fruit.	Use contact insecticide as soon as identified. With a small infestation use aerosol spray. Keep watch for several days and spray again if necessary.
Mealy bugs Small, light pink, stationary sucking insects covered with white, waxy threads. Often seen in dense colonies on tender young growth and tend to hide in areas such as the sheaths of palm leaves.	Suck sap causing plant to wither and die if not cleared promptly.	Use contact or systemic insecticide. Repeat treatment at least three times – every 7 to 10 days.
Red spider mite With eight legs rather than six, this is a proper spider, not an insect and is so minute that it cannot be seen with the naked eye. Usually detected when leaves turn a silvery grey on top, then brown. Plant eventually sheds leaves.	Lives on the undersides of leaves and spins a fine web. Sucks sap, causing discoloration of leaves, leaf drop, and finally death. Thrives in hot weather. May produce a new generation every 16 days. Attacks wilted plants and those not growing vigorously.	Cure by spraying with a miticide or use systemic plant pins. Ensure that your plants never dry out. Use a systemic poison where possible.

Aphids

Red spider mite

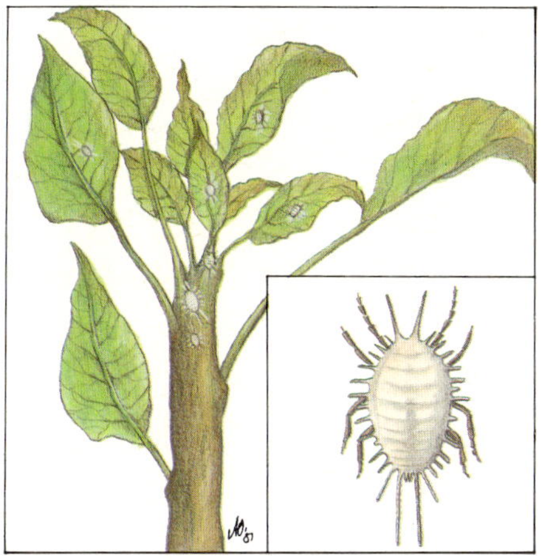

Mealy bugs

PESTS	DAMAGE	CONTROL
Scale insects There are many species of this sucking insect, which lives enclosed in a hard shield. Usually brown, purple or greyish-white. Nymphs live underneath parent's shield and are difficult to destroy. Usually found on stems, next to main veins or on the backs of leaves.	Retard growth and eventually kills the plant.	Difficult to control. Use effective contact insecticide or mineral oil-based insecticide which causes suffocation. Once the insects are dead it should be possible to chip off their empty shells with your thumbnail.
Whitefly Very small, about 3 mm long with four wings, these insects are covered with a white powder and live mainly on the undersides of leaves, rising in clouds when disturbed. Eggs are laid under leaves on short stalks.	Retard growth by sucking sap of plant and eventually causes the plant to die.	Multiplying rapidly, these little insects are very difficult to control. Only insecticides developed specifically for this problem are effective. Check with your local nurseryman for the correct product. Proper application in this situation is critical. Ensure that stated dosage is used accurately. Under- or over-application can cause problems. Spray both sides of leaves as follows: First application. Second application three days later. Third application seven days later. Fourth application seven days later.

Whitefly

Botrytis cinerea

Rust (ground)

Powdery mildew

DISEASES	DAMAGE	CONTROL
Black spot A fungal disease, starting with black spots with yellow borders on older leaves.	Causes leaf drop and finally the death of the plant if not controlled.	Regular spraying programme with contact or systemic fungicide.
Botrytis cinerea This soil-born fungal disease initially causes small brown circles to form on stems, finally causing them to rot.	Causes collapse of stems and finally of plant. Should not occur if proper potting soil is used.	Use systemic fungicide as a soil drench.
Powdery mildew A powdery grey-white growth develops on younger parts of plants and then spreads to the rest of the plant.	The growth can, if left untreated, cause the plant to die.	Regular spray programme with contact or systemic fungicide. This cannot undo the damage, but new growth will be clean.
Rust (ground) Caused by a fungus, it appears in different form from species to species. Produces raised fluffy rings of red or brown or forms white, dry, dead patches on leaves. A summer rather than a winter problem, it develops in hot, humid conditions.	In extreme cases the plant will shed all its leaves and die.	A regular spraying programme, using a systemic fungicide, must be maintained every 7 to 10 days as long as favourable conditions last.

Black spot

Holiday care

Holidays are great for humans but they can spell disaster for indoor plants unless you give some careful thought to their comfort while you are away. There may be a doggy hotel for Rastus and even accommodation for Tibby Cat, but there are no cosy hideaways for your dieffenbachia or your dizygotheca. When going away – unless you have family or a kind neighbour to look after your plants – you need to have a plan of action or you'll be met by a very dreary sight on your return home.

If you have a garden it is wise to leave your house plants outside. All indoor plants should be kept in the shade when out of doors and it is a good idea to sink each pot up to its neck in soil to prevent the wind from drying it out completely. Soaking the ground around the plants before leaving will also help to keep them cool and moist. This way your plants will, under normal circumstances, remain happy for more than a week and with luck there may be rain to keep them going for much longer.

If you have a flat or for some reason you are unable to take your plants into the garden, then try a few of the following ideas:

• Water your plants well just before leaving and cover with a large plastic bag supported by a framework of thin sticks. This should keep the plant happy for 10 days to two weeks.

• Another equally successful method is to form a cocoon made of tinfoil around the pot of each plant. The shiny side should be on the outside to reflect heat away from the plant.

Both these methods are very successful, but you must ensure that the plants are in a cool place, well away from any direct sun.

• An excellent survival method for all container plants, whether inside the house or in the garden, is to fill a bucket or bath with water and then group around it as many plants as possible with long absorbent wicks leading from the tub to each plant. Remember that it is important for the container with water to be higher than the surrounding plants. This method will keep your plants moist until the water source dries up. Check the system a few days before leaving on holiday to ensure that it is functioning properly.

• Many flat gardeners find that a very successful method of keeping plants cool and comfortable is to soak them and then place them in a bath or kitchen sink with masses of wet newspaper packed between them. This helps maintain moisture and humidity.

None of these methods is difficult and will certainly save you having to buy new plants after every holiday. If you can find someone to water your plants thoroughly just once while you are away, topping up the water in the reservoir to keep wicks going or rewetting the newspaper around pots in the bath after about 14 days, you will be able to enjoy a carefree holiday for a month or more.

Keeping plants moist over holidays

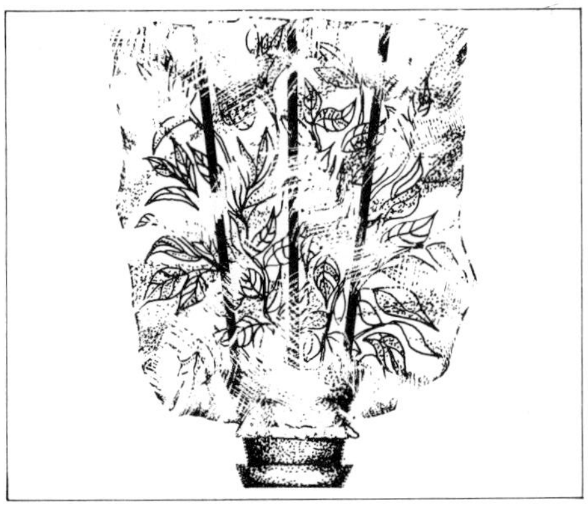

• Plastic bag method

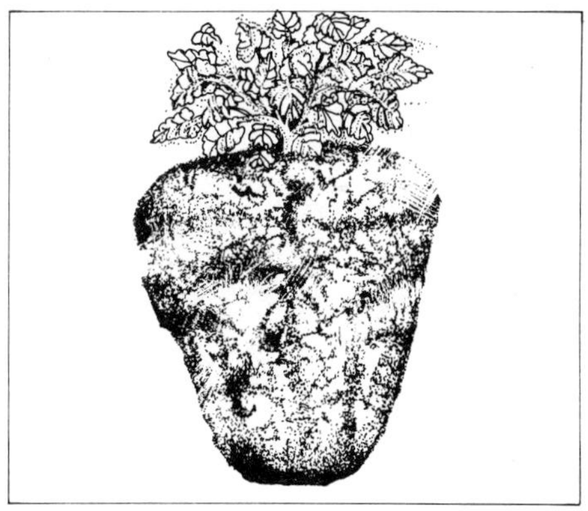

• Tinfoil method

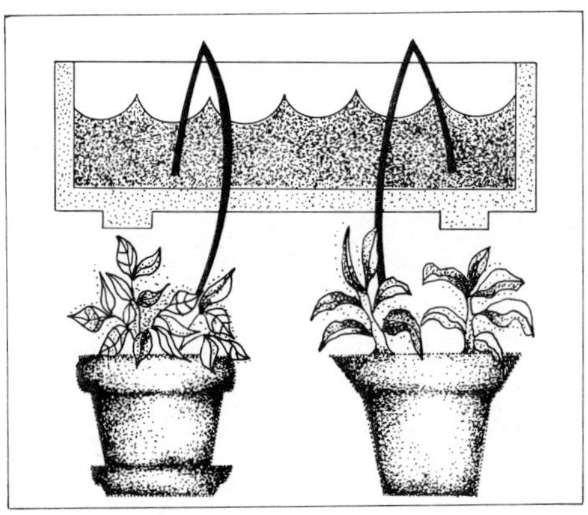

• Bucket and wick method

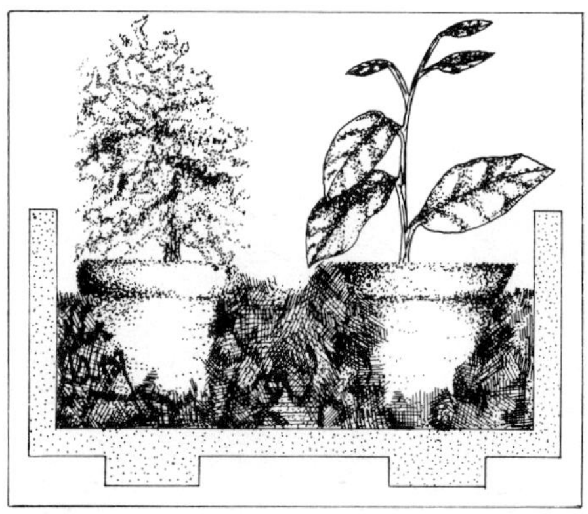

• Newspaper method

Positioning of plants

Listed below is a variety of plants which may be used for specific purposes and under different light conditions in the home. We have also supplied a list of the 10 plants we consider the most attractive and successful for indoor cultivation.

Our 10 favourite indoor plants

Aglaonema varieties
Aspidistra elatior
Chamaedorea elegans
Cissus rhombifolia
Howea forsteriana
Plectranthus australis
Rhapis excelsa
Spathiphyllum wallisii
Streptocarpus hybrids
Syngonium podophyllum 'White Butterfly'

Flowering plants

Achimenes hybrids
Aechmea fasciata
Aeschynanthus radicans
Ananas comosus
Anthurium andraeanum
Azalea varieties
Begonia elatior
Begonia maculata
Begonia tuberhybrida
Billbergia varieties
Browallia speciosa
Calceolaria hybrids
Capsicum hybrids
Chrysanthemum indicum hybrids
Columnea microphylla
Cryptanthus hybrids
Cyclamen persicum
Cymbidium hybrids
Episcia cupreata
Eucharis amazonica
Euphorbia pulcherrima
Guzmania lingulata
Hippeastrum varieties
Hoya varieties
Hyacinthus varieties

Streptocarpus hybrid (p. 59)

Kalanchoe blossfeldiana
Kalanchoe tessa
Lachenalia hybrids
Leucojum aestivum
Lilium hybrids
Narcissus hybrids
Narcissus tazetta
Neoregelia carolinae 'Meyendorfii'
Nidularium fulgens
Pachystachys lutea
Primula acaulis
Primula obconica
Roses (mini and micro-mini)
Saintpaulia ionantha
Senecio cruentus hybrids
Sinningia speciosa
Solanum pseudocapsicum
Spathiphyllum 'Mauna Loa'
Spathiphyllum wallisii
Stephanotis floribunda
Streptocarpus hybrids
Thunbergia alata
Tillandsia usneoides
Tulip hybrids
Vriesea mariae

Cissus rhombifolia 'Ellen Danica' (p. 86)

Zygocactus truncatus

Bulbs

Achimenes hybrids
Begonia tuberhybrida
Caladium hortulanum varieties
Cyclamen persicum
Hippeastrum varieties
Hyacinthus varieties
Lachenalia hybrids
Leucojum aestivum
Lilium hybrids
Narcissus hybrids
Narcissus tazetta
Sinningia speciosa
Tulip hybrids

Temporary colour plants

Anthurium varieties
Azalea varieties
Begonia elatior
Browallia speciosa
Caladium hortulanum varieties
Cyclamen persicum
Cymbidium hybrids
Euphorbia pulcherrima
Kalanchoe blossfeldiana
Narcissus hybrids
Pachystachys lutea
Primula acaulis
Primula obconica
Roses (mini and micro-mini)
Senecio cruentus hybrids
Streptocarpus hybrids
Zygocactus truncatus

Throwaway colour plants

Browallia speciosa
Calceolaria herbeohybrida
Chrysanthemum indicum hybrids
Hyacinthus varieties
Leucojum aestivum
Lilium hybrids
Narcissus hybrids
Narcissus tazetta
Primula varieties
Roses (mini and micro-mini)
Senecio cruentus hybrids
Solanum varieties
Thunbergia alata
Tulip hybrids

Bromeliads

Aechmea varieties
Ananas comosus varieties
Billbergia varieties
Cryptanthus hybrids
Guzmania varieties
Neoregelia carolinae varieties
Nidularium fulgens
Tillandsia varieties
Vriesea varieties

Chrysanthemum indicum (p. 40)

Miniature rose (p. 55)

Cyclamen persicum (p. 42)

Hippeastrum variety (p. 63)

Trailing/climbing plants
Achimenes hybrids
Aeschynanthus radicans
Callisia elegans
Ceropegia woodii
Chlorophytum comosum varieties
Cissus antarctica
Cissus rhombifolia
Columnea microphylla
Episcia cupreata
Hedera helix varieties
Hoya varieties
Philodendron scandens
Plectranthus australis
Saxifraga stolonifera
Scindapsus aureus varieties
Thunbergia alata
Tillandsia usneoides
Tradescantia varieties
Zebrina pendula
Zygocactus truncatus

Cacti/succulents
Aeonium arboreum 'Nigrum'
Agave victoriae-reginae
Cephalocereus senilis
Echeveria elegans
Echinopsis multiplex
Euphorbia varieties
Kalanchoe blossfeldiana
Kalanchoe tessa
Kalanchoe tomentosa
Lithops varieties
Mammillaria varieties
Rebutia varieties
Sedum morganianum
Sedum rubrotinctum
Senecio rowleyanus
Zygocactus truncatus

Colourful foliage plants
Begonia rex 'Merry Christmas'
Caladium hortulanum varieties
Calathea makoyana
Calathea picturata
Calathea zebrina

Cryptanthus hybrid (p. 72)

Codiaeum varieties
Coleus varieties
Cordyline fruticosa varieties
Dieffenbachia varieties
Dracaena varieties
Hedera helix 'Golddust'
Hypoestes sanguinolenta
Maranta leuconeura kerchoviana
Peperomia griseo-argentea
Peperomia obtusifolia varieties
Philodendron 'Burgundy'
Pisonia brunonia 'Variegata'
Pleomele reflexa variegata
Sansevieria varieties
Schefflera arboricola
Zebrina pendula 'Quadricolor'

Foliage plants
Adiantum varieties
Aechmea fasciata
Aglaonema varieties
Alocasia amazonica
Arecastrum romanzoffianum
Asparagus varieties
Aspidistra elatior
Asplenium nidus
Begonia 'Black Beauty'
Begonia 'Cleopatra'
Begonia maculata
Begonia masoniana
Begonia rex
Caladium hortulanum varieties
Callisia elegans
Ceropegia woodii
Chamaedorea elegans
Chamaedorea seifritzii
Chlorophytum comosum varieties
Chrysalidocarpus lutescens
Cissus rhombifolia
Codiaeum varieties
Coffea arabica
Cordyline fruticosa varieties
Cyrtomium falcatum
Davallia varieties
Dieffenbachia amoena
Dizygotheca elegantissima
Dracaena varieties
Eucharis amazonica
Fatshedera lizei
Fatsia japonica
Ficus benjamina
Ficus elastica 'Decora'
Ficus elastica 'Europa'
Ficus indica
Ficus lyrata
Fittonia verschaffeltii
Fittonia verschaffeltii argyroneura 'Nana'
Guzmania lingulata
Hedera helix varieties
Howea belmoreana
Hypoestes sanguinolenta
Microlepia speluncae
Monstera deliciosa
Nephrolepis exaltata
Nephrolepis exaltata 'Bostoniensis'
Nidularium fulgens
Pellaea rotundifolia
Peperomia scandens
Philodendron hastatum
Philodendron scandens
Philodendron selloum
Phoenix roebelenii
Pilea cadierei
Plectranthus australis
Pleomele varieties
Polyscias fruticosa 'Ming'
Pteris cretica
Pteris ensiformis
Pteris tremula
Rhapis excelsa
Sansevieria varieties
Saxifraga stolonifera
Schefflera actinophylla
Schefflera arboricola
Scindapsus aureus
Selaginella varieties
Soleirolia soleirolii
Spathiphyllum varieties
Stereospernum danielle
Syngonium podophyllum 'Emerald Green'
Tradescantia varieties
Yucca elephantipes
Zebrina pendula

Echeveria species (p. 131)

Hypoestes sanguinolenta (p. 98)

Asplenium nidus (p. 116)

Platycerium bifurcatum (p. 120)

Ferns
Adiantum varieties
Asplenium nidus
Cyrtomium falcatum
Davallia varieties
Microlepia speluncae
Nephrolepis exaltata
Nephrolepis exaltata 'Bostoniensis'
Pellaea rotundifolia
Pteris cretica
Pteris ensiformis 'Evergemensis'
Pteris tremula

Plants for low-light positions
Aglaonema varieties
Aspidistra elatior

Chamaedorea elegans (p. 123)

Billbergia varieties
Chamaedorea elegans
Chlorophytum comosum varieties
Cissus varieties
Coffea arabica
Dracaena varieties
Guzmania lingulata
Howea belmoreana
Nidularium varieties
Peperomia scandens
Sansevieria varieties

Dracaena fragrans 'Massangeana' (p. 91, 92)

Spathiphyllum varieties
Syngonium podophyllum 'White Butterfly'

Form or accent plants
Arecastrum romanzoffianum
Aspidistra elatior
Asplenium nidus
Beaucarnea recurvata
Bromeliad varieties
Chamaedorea elegans
Chrysalidocarpus lutescens
Codiaeum varieties
Coffea arabica
Cordyline fruticosa varieties
Cymbidium hybrids
Dieffenbachia varieties
Dizygotheca elegantissima
Dracaena varieties
Fatshedera lizei
Fatsia japonica
Ficus varieties
Howea belmoreana
Monstera deliciosa
Philodendron selloum
Phoenix roebelenii
Polyscias fruticosa 'Ming'
Rhapis excelsa
Sansevieria varieties
Schefflera actinophylla
Schefflera arboricola
Ti-plants (*Yucca* and *Dracaena* varieties)

Plants for height
Arecastrum romanzoffianum
Begonia maculata
Chrysalidocarpus lutescens
Dracaena varieties
Ficus benjamina
Ficus elastica
Ficus indica
Ficus lyrata
Howea belmoreana
Monstera deliciosa
Philodendron selloum
Rhapis excelsa
Ti-plants (*Yucca* and *Dracaena* varieties)

Palms
Arecastrum romanzoffianum
Chamaedorea elegans
Chrysalidocarpus lutescens
Howea belmoreana
Phoenix roebelenii
Rhapis excelsa

Low-growing plants
Cryptanthus bivittatus 'Minor'
Episcia cupreata
Fittonia verschaffeltii
Fittonia verschaffeltii argyroneura 'Nana'
Hypoestes sanguinolenta
Pilea cadierei
Selaginella varieties
Soleirolia soleirolii
Tradescantia mini-varieties

Plants for bathrooms
Aglaonema commutatum 'Pseudobracteatum'
Aglaonema crispum 'Silver Queen'
Aspidistra elatior
Begonia elatior
Chamaedorea elegans
Chamaedorea seifritzii
Chlorophytum comosum varieties

Howea belmoreana (p. 126)

Cissus rhombifolia
Cissus rhombifolia 'Ellen Danica'
Howea belmoreana
Philodendron scandens
Pteris tremula
Scindapsus aureus varieties
Spathiphyllum wallisii
Syngonium podophyllum 'White Butterfly'
Tradescantia varieties

Directory of plants

1. Flowering plants

Achimenes hybrid

Achimenes hybrids
Hot-water plant

Habit: Growing from the top, sides and bottom of baskets, achimenes form bright pompons of colour. Long, tubular, five-petalled flowers show up well against dark green leaves from late summer until April. Flower colours vary from white and pink to violet-blue and scarlet. Allow the plants to dry out after flowering and finally wrap in newspaper and put away in a warm dry spot for winter. Take them out in September, water and leave hanging until they shoot.

Soil: Use three parts peat moss to one part river sand and one part well-rotted manure.

Light: Bright and airy position but no sun.

Humidity: Thrive in humid conditions but grow well even in hot, dry areas if kept moist and misted at night and in the morning.

Watering: Keep moist but not soggy.

Feeding: Liquid fertiliser weekly, at one-eighth normal strength.

Propagation: Seed in early spring or by division, also in spring.

Uses: Ideal for colour under pergolas and on stoeps.

Varieties: *A. grandiflora* (Mexico) with large reddish purple flowers on 25 cm long stems; *A. coccinea* (Caribbean area) with scarlet blooms on 25 cm long trailing stems; *A. longiflora* (Central America) is a small variety with 18 cm long stems and small violet-blue flowers; *A. alba,* a white variety, is also available. Enquire about the latest hybrids at your garden centre.

TIP: Achimenes have a rather strange habit worth knowing about to encourage growth in spring. If slow to shoot after hibernation, plunge the basket into hot water – something that would kill most other plants, but which sets up the achimenes' growth pattern – hence its common name, hot-water plant.

Aeschynanthus radicans

Aeschynanthus micranthus

Aeschynanthus radicans
Lipstick plant

Habit: Flowering from spring well into summer over a period of several weeks, this South-East Asian beauty is well named – it becomes covered in bright red, two-lipped flowers with yellow throats, which emerge from purplish tube-like calyxes. With trailing stems of up to 90 cm or more, this floriferous beauty is ideal for adding colour indoors. Provides a beautiful display when several plants are grown together in a pot or basket.

Soil: Loam and peat moss in equal parts or a loose bromeliad-type mixture with charcoal pieces is ideal.

Light: Best possible without direct sun.

Humidity: Thrives in areas with a relatively high humidity, doing best in greenhouses on the Highveld.

Watering: Needs ample water, preferably softened to a pH of 4,0-4,5.

Feeding: Feed fortnightly from September to February with liquid fertiliser.

Propagation: Tip and stem cuttings about 10 cm long.

Uses: Ideal basket plant for bright places.

Varieties: There are a great number of varieties available, some blooming earlier than others and some with slightly different flowers, leaf forms and colours. They are rarely available by name, but *A. radicans* 'Variegata', a variety with white flecks in the leaves, is found quite often. Of the older varieties, *A. trichosporum* 'Pulchrum' has green sepals. *A. speciosus*, known as the basket vine, has waxy scarlet flowers which are tipped with orange, and blooms in late winter. *A. micranthus* has red, bugle-shaped flowers on slender stems and glossy leaves.

TIP: After a winter rest period, allow the plant to dry out for about three weeks to stimulate it back into flower. Then water and feed immediately to encourage lush growth.

Anthurium andraeanum

Anthurium scherzeranum

Anthurium varieties
Flamingo plant

Habit: There are nearly 600 classified species of anthurium but the many hybrids of the exotic Costa Rican plant *A. andraeanum* are the most popular and best known. Each plant produces five to six colourful palette-shaped spathes (flowers) annually, often 13-25 cm in size. They stay alive for many months if left on the plant. Colours range from white and cream to soft pinks, blood-red, bicolours, tricolours and even doubles. Its shiny, dark green, heart-shaped leaves are also attractive. These slow-growing plants are expensive because they take three years to reach flowering stage.

Soil: Anthuriums enjoy a very light soil with plenty of bark included in the mix. A good mix should include two parts good garden loam; four parts bark (otherwise coarse, clean river sand or fine pebbles); four parts peat moss (imported where possible); two parts of either horse or cow manure which has been well rotted or mushroom compost. The mixture should be very open and if squeezed in your hand should fall apart when you open your hand. Include 1 kg bone meal or superphosphate for every 12 litres volume of the mixture. A pH of between 5,00 and 6,00 is important. When planting, ensure that the crown is not covered with soil. Roots that open up due to the crown lifting should be covered with sphagnum moss.

Light: Anthuriums enjoy 60-70 per cent filtered sun or extremely bright light. They do well in north-facing rooms with filter curtains.

Humidity: High humidity – spray daily with rainwater if possible. *A. andraeanum* enjoys an average temperature above 20 °C and *A. scherzeranum* and *A. crystallinum* above 15 °C.

Watering: Anthuriums enjoy regular watering about three times a week, but ensure that drainage is good or their fleshy, orchid-like roots will rot.

Feeding: Use a liquid food regularly throughout their growing season from August to April.

Propagation: Divide when the plant becomes too large for its pot and grow offsets in 7 cm deep pots. If the plant becomes too large for its pot, the top may be cut off a few centimetres above ground level and planted to form a new plant while the base root system will continue to produce offsets.

Uses: Blooming on and off throughout the year, this is an ideal colour plant for a home where the correct humidity can be maintained.

Varieties: In addition to the colourful *A. andraeanum* hybrids mentioned in the introduction, *A. crystallinum* is chosen for its attractive heart-shaped, velvety green foliage which has silver veins, while *A. scherzeranum,* probably the best choice for home use, has rather narrower dark green leaves about 20 cm long with shiny wax-like, round scarlet spathes and a prominent, curled orange spadix. It also produces many more flowers during a season than most anthuriums.

TIP: When transplanting, be careful not to damage the roots, ensuring that they have not stuck to the side of the pot. If they have, separate painstakingly.

Azalea variety

Azalea varieties (*Rhododendron* varieties)

Habit: Though they will not live indoors indefinitely, these prolific bloomers make excellent temporary house plants while in flower. Azaleas are available in a variety of whites, pinks and cerises, and there is also a very popular pink-and-white bicolour. Often these charming little shrubs are so covered in flowers that it is almost impossible to see the leaves. When small, pinch back the tips to improve shape and bushiness. After flowering return to the garden or patio until flowering again, or plant in the garden.

Soil: Known as acid-soil loving plants, it is important to include at least one third peat moss, preferably the imported variety, and some sand with their soil. If using commercial potting soil add extra peat moss to the mix. Ensure good drainage with coarse sand at the base of the pot.

Light: Give as much light as possible to ensure continued flowering. Azaleas should have at least a few hours of morning sun. Buds will not open in dark positions.

Humidity: Average.

Watering: Soak thoroughly then rewater when the surface soil begins to dry out. Always do a finger test to find when watering is necessary. During a hot summer, particularly if windy, this may be necessary twice a day. Cover soil with a mulch of peat moss during the flowering period to retain moisture. Azaleas must never dry out.

Feeding: During bud formation from March to September, plants are best fed with a fertiliser of NPK, ratio 2:1:3, while during their growth period use 3:1:2.

Propagation: Tip cuttings about 10 cm long.

Uses: Hard to beat where colour is needed in bright situations as they flower for a long time. Ideal for use on table tops and counters.

Varieties: Large azaleas are not suitable for indoor growth, but there are many mini-varieties, such as the Belgian dwarf azaleas *(A. indica)* and their named hybridised varieties which are excellent.

TIP: Azaleas have a very shallow root system, so the shape of their container is important. This should be shallow rather than deep, but deeper than bowl-shape. Due to the shallowness of the roots it is important never to cultivate ground covers or other plants around them. Even pulling weeds may damage their roots, so keep soil covered in a protective peat blanket (mulch).

Azalea indica

Above, left and right, and below: *Begonia elatior* 'Schwabenland'

Begonia elatior

Habit: One of the throwaway plants one usually buys in bud and enjoys while in bloom before discarding, for it will not flower the following year. Take cuttings to make new plants. This is a very attractive modern begonia variety, with masses of lovely colourful flowers about the size of a rand coin. To keep flowering, remove dead heads and do not allow seeds to form.

Soil: Best grown in well-aerated soil. Mix equal parts of leaf mould, peat moss and sharp sand with only a small portion of garden loam. Ensure good drainage.

Light: Good light is needed or buds will not open and colours will not be appreciated.

Humidity: A little above average.

Watering: Allow the surface of the soil to dry between good waterings. Begonias have fleshy stems that store water so should not be overwatered, especially if grown in poor light.

Feeding: Liquid food monthly.

Propagation: Tip cuttings 10 cm long.

Uses: *B. elatior* is a fine colour plant for bright positions and makes an excellent gift.

Varieties: Available in soft shades of lemon, pink, orange, pale and dark red, and white. South Africa's larger nurseries mostly grow *B. elatior* 'Schwabenland' which is almost identical to *B. elatior*. It has similar colours but grows taller.

Begonia maculata
Angel wing begonia

Habit: This begonia and a number of other similar varieties of the fibrous rooted type which grow on long canes, are all known by the same common name – angel wings. *B. maculata* has dark green leaves with silver spots and red undersides, but some of the others have plain green leaves. Popular in the early years of this century, these vigorous 1 m tall shrub begonias have once again become very fashionable. This is not surprising, for they are attractive even without their clusters of graceful pink flowers which bloom on and off throughout the year, but mainly in summer. They are named for the way their pairs of lance-shaped leaves, with rounded lobes, are arranged in pairs, very much like angel wings. They must be pinched back to encourage bushiness and regularly cut down to about 45 cm to encourage the development of more canes.

Soil: Use commercial potting soil with some peat added, or make your own mixture with equal parts of garden loam, peat, humus or bark and some river sand. Ensure that the pot is well drained with a good layer of river sand at the bottom.

Light: To ensure that the plants flower, try to give them at least four hours' sun per day. Begonias do best in north-facing windows.

Humidity: Medium.

Watering: Soak thoroughly and then allow the surface to become almost dry before watering again. Excessive leaf loss is an indication of overwatering. Give even less water during winter months.

Feeding: Fertilise with liquid food every month or two.

Propagation: Use 10 cm long cuttings of non-flowering tips or stem sections dipped in hormone powder and plant in peat moss or peat moss and sand mixture.

Uses: Best seen alone, they make attractive but not too heavy form plants. They look attractive in Chinese-type ceramic pots and in brass containers.

Varieties: *B.* 'Corallina de Lucerna' is a taller variety, growing up to 2 m, with coral flowers and green leaves with white spots. *B. glaucophylla* produces clusters of orange flowers amongst its light green leaves.

Begonia maculata

Above: *Begonia semperflorens* in pink (top) and vodka

Begonia semperflorens
Wax begonia

Habit: The most widely grown of the begonias, this delightful fibrous-rooted variety is generally sold as a bedding plant but does very well in pots and bowls in bright areas that get some sun, such as a windowsill or stoep table. Forms include bronze leaf and green leaf types with either white, pink or red flowers.

Soil: Commercial potting soil is ideal, otherwise make your own mixture of equal parts of compost, peat moss and river sand with just a little good garden loam added.

Light: Needs exceedingly good light, preferably with some morning sun.

Humidity: Slightly above average.

Watering: Keep moist but not soggy. Water when soil surface becomes slightly dry.

Feeding: Liquid food monthly.

Propagation: Seed.

Uses: A cheerful plant for bright, sunny areas such as stoeps.

TIP: These very versatile plants may be cut right back when they stop flowering and will continue blooming happily for another season.

Above: *Browallia speciosa* in white (top) and violet

Browallia speciosa
Bush violet

Habit: An attractive shrubby plant with white-throated blue flowers and shiny deep green leaves. It is one of the easiest plants to grow indoors and should be started from seed and then transplanted to pots. Growing tips should be pinched back regularly when young to develop bushy well-branched plants. Remove dead flowers regularly for long display during spring and summer. Does not flower when days get shorter.

Soil: Transplant from seed trays into commercial potting soil or a loamy garden soil mix which includes at least one third compost.

Light: Very bright light with little direct sun.

Humidity: Average or a little higher.

Watering: Keep moist, but the soil surface may dry out slightly.

Feeding: Feed fortnightly with organic liquid food or the new powder form, slow-release fertilisers.

Propagation: Sow seed in September for summer flowering and February for winter flowering. Winter blooms do not last as long as those in summer.

Uses: Excellent colour plant for pots alone or mixed with foliage plants. Its slightly drooping stems make it ideal for hanging baskets.

Varieties: Available with white, blue or violet flowers.

Calceolaria herbeohybrida
Slipper plant

Habit: Looking rather like ladies' slippers, with a pouch-like lower lip, the slightly speckled flowers cluster densely at the top of their stems to form an umbrella of colour. Under cool, airy conditions the flowers last quite a long time. Calceolarias are annuals and should be thrown away after flowering.

Soil: Calceolarias enjoy a loose, friable soil which includes at least one third compost and some river sand.

Light: Bright light but no sun.

Humidity: Average, but raise if buds drop.

Watering: Keep moist at all times but not soggy.

Feeding: Feed fortnightly with a balanced liquid fertiliser.

Propagation: Grow by seed annually.

Uses: Excellent, neat colour plants which make fine gifts. Ideal for windowsills or as a centrepiece.

Varieties: Calceolarias are available in a wide range of colours: yellow and brown, bronze, pink, red, orange and maroon.

Calceolaria herbeohybrida

Capsicum hybrids
Ornamental pepper

Habit: Colourful peppers are extremely popular for indoor decoration. Most are bushy and compact, usually about 30 cm tall. The plants produce insignificant flowers, but these are followed by attractive fruits in a variety of shapes, some upright, long and cone-shaped, some pendulous and some globular. They are usually coloured bright yellow, purple or red. They are both profuse and long lasting, keeping up to 12 weeks before fruits wrinkle and drop off. Regarded as throwaway plants, they are generally discarded at that point.

Soil: Use a loamy mixture with equal parts garden soil, compost and river sand.

Light: Bright light, including several hours of direct sun, otherwise plants suffer leaf drop.

Humidity: Average.

Watering: Allow the surface of the potting mixture to dry between good waterings.

Feeding: Organic liquid food fortnightly.

Propagation: Annually by seed but usually bought in fruit at nurseries.

Uses: Attractive form and colour specimens for bright positions in the home.

Varieties: 'Aurora', a compact dwarf with buff-coloured fruits changing from purple to orange and red. Attractive at all stages, 'Holiday Cheer' has round fruit shaded through several colours before ultimately turning bright red, rather like a Jerusalem cherry. 'Fireworks' has cream-coloured, cone-shaped fruit turning to red, often having both colours on a semispreading bush at the same time.

Below: *Capsicum* 'Holiday Cheer'
Bottom: *Capsicum* 'Aurora'

Chrysanthemum indicum hybrids
Mums

Habit: Temporary house plants, chrysanthemums are probably the most popular flowering indoor plant in South Africa. With massed flowers totally covering the heads of the upright stalks, they offer a splendid display. After flowering they may be planted into the garden.

Soil: Chrysanthemums prefer well-aerated soil containing at least one third compost or other organic matter and some river sand.

Light: Require bright light or even some sun for flowers to keep opening over a long period. Under cool conditions and bright light they may flower for up to six weeks.

Humidity: Average.

Watering: Water well then allow the surface soil to dry out before rewatering. Do not overwater or allow to stand in a saucer of water. If they wilt, plunge the entire pot into a basin of water until thoroughly soaked. Allow to drain and they will recover.

Feeding: Liquid food fortnightly.

Below, left to right: *Chrysanthemum indicum* hybrids in pink, yellow and orange

Above, left and right: *Chrysanthemum indicum* hybrids in different colours and settings

Propagation: As house plants these are generally bought at nurseries or garden centres, for to produce the compact plants often bearing 20 or more blooms requires special production techniques involving artificial shortening and lengthening of days. When buying, always ensure that the flowers are open or well out or else they will not bloom satisfactorily.

Uses: They may be used as single specimens or three to five pots may be grouped together in a basket, or even displayed in troughs with other plants such as ivies.

TIP: Chrysanthemums should not be thrown away after flowering. Cut down to a few centimetres high and plant in the garden where they will give you a super display and provide masses of cut flowers the following autumn. However, because they are in the open, they will not again form the compact plants developed under greenhouse conditions. Chrysanthemums normally grow rather tall, but if you plant out your house plant near autumn, it may develop flowers on stubby stems the first year, regaining its normal growth pattern the following season.

Columnea microphylla
Goldfish vine

Habit: This subtropical beauty – ideal for our more humid regions – is not easy to grow inland except in green- or shade houses, but is well worth the trouble if you succeed. With cascading woolly-leafed stems which become covered with bright scarlet flowers, it is a delight from April to October. The flowers are followed by striking white berries. Bracts should be pruned when berries are over to encourage branching.

Soil: Basically an epiphyte, it enjoys an open peat mixture, which includes some commercial potting soil and river sand, small pieces of charcoal and sphagnum moss.

Light: Columneas are shade lovers that enjoy bright but filtered sunlight and do surprisingly well in artificial light.

Humidity: They prefer a humidity of over 50 per cent and in dry areas pots should be placed on humidity trays. Spray baskets with water at room temperature only – cold water causes ugly marks on the leaves.

Watering: Water freely during the growth period, less during the rest period.

Feeding: Give doses of liquid fertiliser weekly, except during the rest period.

Propagation: Use small cuttings of unflowered shoots in September.

Uses: Superb specimen plant for hanging baskets or for pots placed on high walls where it can cascade successfully.

Varieties: *C. microphylla* has dark green succulent leaves; *C. microphylla* 'Variegata' has pale green foliage with a white edge; and *C. microphylla* 'Stavanger' also has a variegated but slightly darker leaf than *C. microphylla* 'Variegata' and its flowers are longer. *C. hirsuitissima* is very similar to *C. microphylla*, but has slightly larger leaves.

Columnea hirsuitissima

Cyclamen persicum varieties

Cyclamen persicum

Habit: With lovely flowers which look like butterflies hovering on succulent stems above attractive, round, grey-green leaves mottled with white, these bright and exquisitely coloured plants are not the throwaway plants many people consider them to be. Repot each year to obtain really large specimen plants (see tip below).

Soil: Cyclamen enjoy a well-aerated soil mix including equal parts of garden loam, compost and river sand. Commercial potting soil is ideal.

Light: They thrive in bright light but cool positions such as a south window.

Cyclamen persicum

Humidity: Average.

Watering: This is most important. Water regularly, but never allow the soil to be soggy or the corm will rot. Water under the leaves but never on the crown. Good drainage is vital.

Feeding: Feed regularly with good liquid food or the newly available special slow-release bulb food throughout the growing season, until the leaves die down.

Propagation: Seeds and tubers.

Uses: They make fine gifts and are extremely useful for brightening coffee tables, bookcase shelves, desk tops and bright windowsills.

Varieties: Cyclamen are available in a range of lovely whites, lilacs, pinks and brilliant reds. A wonderful little miniature variety, which is only 15 cm tall, looks exactly the same as the standard variety, but is even more prolific. They are magnificent grouped in single colours in large bowls.

TIP: Cyclamen will give you joy for many years. Do not discard them after flowering. Rather continue watering until November, then put under a tree in the garden until January or February by which time they will have lost all their foliage. At that point, place the pots on their sides in the garage so that they will not be watered until revived again in autumn. They should be repotted after removing soil from the corms, while retaining as many roots as possible. Plant in soil with the top third of the plant exposed and start watering again to bring back to full growth.

Cymbidium hybrid

Miniature cymbidium

Cymbidium hybrids

Habit: Among the most beautiful of orchids, the cymbidium is by far the easiest to grow. In fact, it is the only worthwhile variety for the average gardener without a greenhouse. Their rarity used to give them a certain mystique, but now they are multiplied rapidly in laboratories by the vegetative meristemming method, making them freely available. Fragile though the blooms may seem, the plants are tough and may be handled without bruising. A favourite for corsages because of their ethereal loveliness, the tall flower spikes seem to float above lovely dense and arching strap-like leaves.

Soil: The growing medium is most important. Most garden centres sell a special cymbidium mix, but you can blend your own. Your mix must be light, drain well yet hold moisture, have a pH value of 4,5-6,00 and be firm enough to support the plant in an upright position. A leading South African grower finds pine needles with a small quantity of polystyrene granules an excellent mix, but most people prefer to use blends of some of the following: chunks of pine bark, charcoal, peach pips, rice husks and even peanut shells, coarse gravel or sand.

Light: Cymbidiums may take a little morning sun but generally prefer filtered sun all day or extremely bright conditions. Grow under trees which provide filtered sun for most of the year, then enjoy them in the home when in bloom.

Humidity: Water around the plants to increase humidity, for cymbidiums like an above-average humidity of up to 40 per cent.

Watering: This is most important. They should never be allowed to dry out and in summer this may mean watering every day. If very hot and dry it is a good idea to mist the leaves as well.

Feeding: Orchids need regular feeding, preferably fortnightly but at least monthly. Special fertilisers are available for use at specific times: during growth periods, when forming buds and another for in between. If that sounds like a lot of work, many experts believe that all that is necessary is merely to use a liquid pot plant food which includes micro-elements.

Propagation: By division of plants. This should be done every two years, or repot into bigger pots.

Uses: They are exciting decorating plants. Cymbidiums can bloom for up to three months. Buy or bring them into the house when buds are half-open and you will enjoy the opening of each flower.

Varieties There are two groups of hybrids – the so-called standard cymbidiums and the 'miniatures'. Standard cymbidiums have tall spikes of flowers and each bloom is 10 cm across. The mini-varieties' flowers and foliage are about half the size. They come in a beautiful range of colours from orange and red to pinks and other pastel shades, as well as yellow and green. Trailing mini-varieties have now become very popular.

Cymbidium hybrid

TIP: Yellowing leaves, which feel dry, could mean a variety of things: you are overwatering or overfeeding, the soil mixture is badly drained or the growing medium is old and needs replacing. If the heart of the plant starts going black and new shoots rot, treat with a fungicide. Spotted or striped leaves usually indicate a virus and, as no treatment is available for this malady, the plant should be thrown away.

Trailing cymbidium

Episcia cupreata

Eucharis amazonica

Episcia cupreata
Flame violet

Habit: This tropical beauty is best suited to Natal's subtropical coastal area, but will do well inland if grown on a humidity tray or in a room with a humidifier. Their beautifully patterned, slightly furry, coloured leaves with silvery-green and brown markings are an excellent foil for their bright, orange-red tubular flowers which cover the plant for most of summer and even on into winter. They belong to the African violet family.

Soil: Commercial potting soil is ideal.

Light: Very bright, just short of direct sunlight, otherwise they will not flower.

Humidity: Occasionally mist leaves with water.

Temperature: Extremely sensitive to cold. Do not keep them in areas where the temperature drops to below 18 °C.

Watering: Never allow them to dry out. Water well and then leave until the surface soil becomes dry.

Feeding: Either chemical or organic liquid food fortnightly, after watering.

Propagation: Best done in spring or summer by inserting stolons (plantlets) attached to trailing stems into a tray of river sand. When rooted, cut the 'umbilical cord' and replant. Episcias are best rejuvenated every year as they age very quickly. Keep well watered during propagation.

Uses: Beautiful subjects for low coffee tables and in small hanging baskets.

Eucharis amazonica
Eucharist lily

Habit: Grown as much for its beautiful, broad, dark green, strap-like leaves as for its clusters of attractive pendulous white flowers, this fragrant beauty is very special. Most successful in humid areas, where the temperature does not fall below 13 °C, this lily thrives along the Natal coast. Inland it generally flowers only when it becomes pot-bound.

Soil: Plant bulbs 3 cm below the surface of a rich, porous potting mixture which contains equal parts of soil, peat moss (preferably the imported variety) and river sand. Repot only when really overcrowded.

Light: Happy with a position which is a little less than bright, but which is not too dim.

Humidity: Prefers above-average humidity and in inland areas will certainly benefit from standing on a humidity tray. Regular misting of the leaves also helps.

Watering: Must be kept moist from spring through autumn but in winter it may have brief dry spells between watering. If overwatered, stem rot may occur. Should this happen, treat with systemic fungicide. Clean leaves regularly with a damp cloth.

Feeding: Use liquid food monthly.

Propagation: By bulbs, division of plants and by seed.

Uses: An impressive plant in leaf, it is superb when in flower. Excellent bold accent plant.

Euphorbia pulcherrima

Euphorbia pulcherrima
Poinsettia

Habit: Hybridised and developed into densely flowered, compact little plants, the modern poinsettia has become one of the top selling indoor colour plants. One of the best known symbols of Christmas in Northern Hemisphere countries, they are now, thanks to glasshouse production, also available here in December – and throughout the year. Cheery and bright with large red petals, which are in reality coloured bracts framing an insignificant yellow blossom, they are long lasting. When finished flowering they may be planted into the garden to make excellent neat shrubs in frost-free areas.

Soil: Use commercial potting soil or a well-aerated mix of equal parts of garden loam, compost and river sand.

Light: As bright as possible, otherwise the quality of the colourful bracts deteriorates.

Humidity: Average.

Watering: Poinsettias enjoy being kept moist but not soggy, and the surface of the soil may be allowed to dry out slightly between waterings.

Feeding: Liquid fertiliser monthly.

Propagation: Tip cuttings 8-10 cm long, or stem cuttings double that length.

Uses: Poinsettias make excellent gifts and brighten up coffee tables and bookcases, room dividers, desk tops and indoor gardens.

Varieties: Modern hybrids are available in a variety of shades, including pinks, white, cream and the normal red.

Hoya carnosa
Wax flower

Habit: With waxy blooms, which glisten with honey-sweet drops of nectar, hoyas could easily be mistaken for plastic. This Chinese trailer has unusual, compact, parasol-like umbels made up of many tiny star-like flowers with their tips touching. It has leathery, dark green leaves. With strong likes and dislikes, hoyas are happiest when pot-bound and should be repotted only when absolutely necessary (see tip below).

Soil: Porous, sandy loam, with a pH 6,5-7,0. Include some broken pieces of charcoal.

Light: Bright but no direct sun.

Humidity: Low.

Watering: Water well during the active growing spell and when in flower, but tail off during winter.

Feeding: Liquid fertiliser fortnightly, particularly as it ages, for they flower more the older they get. Sprinkle bone phosphate on the soil around the plant twice during the growing season.

Propagation: Between November and January, take cuttings of young shoots with a terminal bud and a pair of leaves, but which are slightly woody at the base.

Uses: Decorative, night-fragrant hoyas look good on light trellises and in baskets.

Varieties: *H. carnosa* 'Variegata' has leaves with broad cream borders with a faint tinge of pink. *H. bella* is a miniature variety.

TIP: Very sensitive to the direction of light, hoyas should be left in one position and not turned, particularly when in bud, otherwise they will drop their buds. Once happy, leave well alone – they hate being tampered with. Do not remove the spurs on which hoya flowers bloom when cleaning the plant or you will lose future flowers.

Hoya bella

Impatiens 'New Guinea' hybrids

Habit: Although similar to the popular busy Lizzie in many ways, nonetheless the New Guinea impatiens is a different plant. It offers a variety of differently variegated leaves, with various blends of green, yellow, pink and bronze in combinations with different coloured flowers, ranging from pink and lilac to orange and dark red. These hybrids also enjoy more light than their cousins, with the leaves turning green in too much shade.

Soil: Commercial potting soil is ideal.

Humidity: Thrives in either humid or dry conditions, provided it is well watered.

Light: Must have about four hours' sun to retain the attractive leaf colours, but too much sun will result in less attractive flowers and may even burn them. Try to strike a happy medium.

Watering: Keep well watered. Never allow to dry out.

Feeding: Use liquid food fortnightly during the growing season to keep them healthy and flowering.

Propagation: Cuttings root very easily, particularly if dipped in a root hormone powder.

Uses: Particularly good in indoor gardens where they can be massed. They also look good in large pots in well-lit, sunny positions.

Varieties: There are a huge number of named varieties but most people choose them according to the flower and foliage colour combinations they prefer. The choice is remarkable, with combinations varying from yellow leaves and red flowers to pink-tinged leaves and soft lilac-coloured flowers as well as orange flowers with deep-bronze leaves.

Left and below: *Impatiens* 'New Guinea' hybrids

Impatiens walleriana

Impatiens walleriana **hybrids**

Busy Lizzie

Habit: These charming plants which do so well in the shady garden, also do well as indoor plants in airy windows and particularly on shady stoeps. The modern varieties which trail over the edge of baskets are particularly attractive and become so full of flowers when content with their position that hardly a leaf is seen.

Soil: Impatiens thrive in most soils – commercial potting soil is ideal.

Light: Although they enjoy shade, impatiens can take some early morning or late afternoon sun and do best when given bright light for most of the day. They need a moderate temperature and will start flowering much later on the cold Highveld than they do in subtropical climates where they flower virtually non-stop.

Humidity: Impatiens enjoy high humidity but thrive even in hot, dry inland areas.

Watering: Impatiens need to be kept moist constantly, and will even root and grow in water, which is why they are called 'waterfuchsias' in Afrikaans.

Feeding: The most undemanding of flowering plants, impatiens do even better when given a little liquid food as encouragement on a regular fortnightly basis.

Propagation: By cuttings which may be rooted in water before planting, or by seed, but that is more difficult.

Uses: Few plants are more desirable in places where constant colour is needed. Attractive either in pots or in hanging baskets.

TIP: To increase stocks, place cuttings in a glass or bottle of water where they will root rapidly. When ready, plant out into good commercial potting soil and they will soon develop into neat little plants.

Impatiens walleriana in a bright pink

Kalanchoe blossfeldiana

Kalanchoe blossfeldiana hybrids

Habit: Although an attractive plant with a compact dome of fleshy green leaves, this succulent's charm is in its tightly clustered heads of orange, red, yellow and salmon-coloured small flowers on upright stems, which colour the plant for nearly two months at a time.

Soil: A fast-draining mixture of river sand and humus soil.

Light: Requires several hours of direct sunlight with bright light for the remainder of the day to flower successfully.

Humidity: Can take a little more humidity than most succulent varieties.

Watering: Enjoys rather dry conditions. Allow to dry in between good waterings.

Feeding: Liquid fertiliser monthly.

Propagation: Tip cuttings and by seed.

Uses: For colour in sun rooms, stoeps and bright indoor areas. Plant out after flowering for it rarely flowers indoors a second time.

Varieties: There are many new hybrid forms in a great variety of colours, including a miniature, *K. blossfeldiana* 'Tom Thumb'.

Below, left to right: *Kalanchoe blossfeldiana* hybrids in bright yellow, orange and red

Kalanchoe tessa

Kalanchoe tessa

Habit: This trailing kalanchoe variety is rapidly growing in popularity and is ideal for use in hanging baskets. It develops long, trailing stems in a matter of months and has attractive small, fleshy leaves. Its charming little flowers have unusual pink to cream petals.

Soil: Grows best in a quick-draining soil mix which includes humus and river sand.

Light: Thrives best in light shade though it can tolerate some direct sunshine in the early morning or late afternoon.

Humidity: Happy with rather more air humidity than most succulent varieties.

Watering: Enjoys fairly dry conditions – allow the soil surface to dry out between good waterings.

Feeding: Liquid fertiliser monthly.

Propagation: By cuttings and seed.

Uses: A most attractive choice for hanging baskets in bright light positions.

Nematanthus gregarius (Hypocyrta glabra)

Goldfish plant

Habit: Strangely, this unusual plant is not very often seen. It has graceful, trailing stems and pairs of succulent-like, glossy oval leaves alternating at right angles to one another. Interspersed between the leaves are yellow, fish-like flowers with slightly puckered mouths which appear throughout the year. It is a quick grower and most rewarding when grown under conditions not dissimilar to those for columneas.

Soil: A quick-draining mix of commercial potting soil with some extra river sand is ideal.

Light: Bright light, near windows in bright rooms or on stoeps.

Humidity: Low to medium.

Watering: Being a succulent-like variety, it enjoys fairly dry conditions.

Feeding: Liquid food monthly during the growing season. Reduce feeding if in good leaf but failing to flower.

Propagation: By cuttings.

Uses: The striking combination of dark green leaves and yellow flowers makes this a most decorative plant for bright positions.

Below and bottom: *Nematanthus gregarius*

Pachystachys lutea
Golden candles

Habit: Although similar to the popular shrimp plant (*Beloperone guttata*) and often called the yellow shrimp, the two are not related. This South American plant has been known since the last century, but it was not until the early 1970s that it gained popularity. It was introduced to South Africa in 1973. In nature it often grows to a couple of metres, but rarely tops 0,5 m in pots. It has glossy, green leaves interspersed with great numbers of upright, bright yellow, flame-shaped bracts, from which minute white florettes peep.

Soil: Add to three parts of imported peat moss one part of garden loam and one part sharp river sand. To prevent the mix from being too acid, add a sprinkling of limestone to keep a pH level of 7,0.

Light: Strong light but no direct sun.

Humidity: Average.

Watering: Ensure good drainage and keep moist at all times. This is one plant that should be overwatered rather than underwatered, but don't overdo it and ensure that it never stands in water.

Feeding: Feed fortnightly with liquid food.

Propagation: It is important to prune these plants back to 15 cm after flowering to stimulate bushiness. When this is done, take 15 cm long tip or stem cuttings.

Uses: A cheerful plant for brightening any room. It is ideal for office counters and desk tops and for mixing with foliage arrangements for colour.

Pachystachys lutea

Primula obconica

Primula varieties
Primrose

Habit: There are a great many varieties of these delicately beautiful but tough plants, yet only two make really good indoor plants: *P. obconica* and *P. acaulis,* a hybrid variety of the original *P. vulgaris.* While *P. acaulis* is a low-growing posy-like variety with rosettes of leaves from which emerge charming little flowers on short stems, *P. obconica* has taller, upright leaves, with even taller stems topped by large umbels of lovely blooms. The little *P. acaulis* comes in a large range of shades including yellow, orange, pink, blue, purple, red and white, while its taller cousins have a more limited range of pink, salmon-pink and pale lavender-blue.

Soil: These plants grow under trees in nature, so ensure that their soil includes quantities of leaf mould. Use equal portions of garden loam and river sand plus a much bigger portion of humus material.

Light: Although primulas enjoy bright light, they should be kept in cool to moderate conditions.

Humidity: Average.

Watering: Although sensitive to drying out, primulas do not like being overwatered. Keep soil moist at all times, but not soggy.

Feeding: Feed fortnightly with liquid food during the growing and flowering seasons.

Propagation: Seed.

Uses: Superb in large, flat bowls in bright entrances and hallways or in small pots for desk and table tops.

TIP: Anyone with a sensitive skin should use gloves or a barrier cream or avoid handling *P. obconica* for, beautiful though it is, its leaves are covered in fine hairs containing an irritant which produces an allergic reaction in many people. (Gloxinias may also cause a rash.)

Above: *Primula acaulis*

Below, left to right: *Primula obconica* in various colours

Roses

French miniature roses

Habit: One can now enjoy the world's favourite flower indoors throughout the year. Dainty and floriferous, these little plants are grown as throwaways, but don't discard them – rather cut them back after they bloom and grow them in your garden.

A product of the eighties, these are new mini- and micro-mini varieties. Both have similar requirements; the only difference is in their size. The mini-varieties are 20-30 cm tall and have 3 cm diameter flowers, the size of a one rand coin, while the micro-minis are only 10 cm tall with flowers the size of a twenty cent coin. To ensure that they bloom for as long as possible, keep removing the dead flowers.

Soil: Commercial potting soil or a mix of equal portions of good garden loam and compost, together with some well-rotted kraal manure. Ensure that the pots are well drained.

Light: As bright a light as possible. Roses grow very well under artificial light, doing best under broad-spectrum fluorescent lamps.

Humidity: Normal.

Watering: Keep soil moist and well drained. Water daily and, when very hot, twice daily. These plants are best watered from a saucer so that they can absorb the water by capillary action, but do not leave them standing in water.

Feeding: Apply a half-strength solution of liquid food weekly.

Propagation: Best left to the professionals.

Uses: Roses make ideal gifts, especially for such occasions as Valentine's Day and Mother's Day. They are beautiful wherever they're placed, but being tiny they are ideal for table and desk tops, and therefore make perfect gifts for hospital patients.

Varieties: These are increasing all the time, but here are a few good choices: mini varieties in a light and dark red, a variety of pinks, including salmon pink, and two yellows; micro-mini varieties in a soft bridal pink, a yellow, and a yellow and red.

TIP: Mini- and micro-mini roses flower on and off throughout the year. It is possible to grow them again indoors if you decide not to grow them in the garden. After flowering, cut back to about 10 cm (with the micro-minis even less) or to approximately three or four fully developed leaves from the base of a shoot. Transplant to a slightly larger pot and within four to six weeks, with fertile soil and favourable conditions, they will bud again. The French miniatures are ideal for bedding and as ground covers under larger roses. Plant them about 30 cm apart.

Left: French miniature rose

Right, top to bottom: Miniature roses in a variety of colours

Above, left and right: *Saintpaulia ionantha*

Saintpaulia ionantha
African violet

Habit: It is always wise to remember the conditions under which African violets were first discovered by Baron Walter von Saint Paul in what used to be Tanganyika (now Tanzania). He found them in a forest near a stream in a pleasantly warm climate with good light and plenty of moisture for the roots and high air humidity. Free-flowering African violets in singles, doubles, ruffled and plain are available in a variety of shades – white and pink, lilac and purple, blue and variegated – and stand out well among their neat collarettes of large and attractive, fuzzy, succulent leaves.

Soil: It is important to have a loose, friable soil which allows for the free movement of air and in which roots may spread easily. The specially prepared commercial African violet soils are best, but if you wish to mix your own, try equal parts of good garden loam and peat moss or sieved leaf mould and coarse river sand. Add a tablespoon of bone phosphate to every two litres of the mixture. African violets are, however, grown in a variety of mediums – even a sterile one such as vermiculite – but then they need regular feeding.

Light: Good, indirect light for growth, stepped up to very bright for flowering. The better the light, the better they will bloom.

Watering: Soak plants thoroughly, then water again when the soil surface is just dry. Use water at room temperature, keeping the plant just moist at all times.

Feeding: Special foods are available which help bring the plants into bloom.

Propagation: Leaf cuttings, division of older plants and seed.

Uses: Displayed either singly or in groups, African violets are essentially specimen plants. They look good on small tables, coffee tables and windowsills. They look particularly attractive when planted into natural rock or hollowed-out cavities in driftwood. Sphagnum moss and maidenhair ferns complement them, and they are ideal foreground plants in terrariums.

TIP: Ensure that the velvety leaves of your African violets are kept clean. It is a fallacy that it is harmful to wet them. Plants benefit from an occasional good dousing with water, but do this in the morning so that they have a good chance to dry out. Use tepid water and never allow them to dry in the sun. Alternatively, you can use a fine brush to dust the leaves.

Senecio cruentus hybrids
Cineraria

Habit: This charming annual makes a beautiful colour plant for the home, providing welcome colour at the end of winter. For mass colour few plants are as cheerful and offer such variety. They produce colourful heads of daisy-like flowers which look as though they have been hand-painted. Cinerarias normally have only one stem but a huge umbel of blooms. They form neat, compact little bushes, no more than 30 cm high.

Soil: Either commercial potting soil or a mix of equal parts good garden loam and peat moss.

Light: Cinerarias tolerate only filtered sun and are best grown near a net-curtained window.

Humidity: Average.

Watering: Keep just moist.

Feeding: When in bud, feed weekly with liquid fertiliser.

Propagation: By seed annually.

Uses: Cinerarias are neat plants and extremely popular for brightening airy but poorly lit windowsills and table tops. Though delicate in appearance, they do not mind draughts.

Varieties: Cinerarias offer a wide variety of colours from white to cornflower blue, a glistening almost navy blue, pinks and purples, bronze and light brown, and carmine and red.

Below and bottom: *Senecio cruentus*

Sinningia speciosa

Sinningia speciosa
Gloxinia

Habit: Velvety gloxinia flowers are so big, bold and bright that they seem almost too big for their pots as they crowd at the top of their hairy 30 cm stems, encircled by large oval, furry, scalloped leaves. The number of flowers – they may bear 20 or more at a time – seems almost too many for the plant. When properly grown, they bloom for a long time.

Soil: A rich but well-aerated potting mixture of equal parts garden loam and river sand, with more than one third compost is ideal (see the chapter on feeding).

Light: Medium light – they do not need very bright light but will not flower well if in too dim a position.

Humidity: Average or a little more.

Watering: Keep moist. The surface soil may dry out a little between waterings, but be careful not to drop water on the leaves as they mark easily.

Feeding: When planting, include a little bone phosphate with your soil and feed fortnightly with a high-phosphate liquid fertiliser diluted to half-strength.

Propagation: By tubers and leaf cuttings as well as seed.

Uses: Gloxinias are highly decorative, and make excellent gifts. They are suitable for coffee tables and desk tops. Though often seen in plant arrangements, they are so spectacular that they look best on their own.

Varieties: Though there are a number of forms suitable for indoors, including *S. cardinalis* (helmet flower), *S. regina* (Cinderella slippers) and some miniatures, they are rarely seen in South Africa.

TIP: After flowering, the leaves die down and watering should be reduced until the plant is dry. Store until the following winter. To start up tubers the following season, place them on top of a tray containing half river sand and half peat which has been moistened. Dampen occasionally until shoots begin to develop. At this point, transfer to small pots, repotting into bigger pots up to 12 cm as the plant grows.

Solanum pseudocapsicum 'New Patterson'

Solanum pseudocapsicum
Jerusalem cherry

Habit: This cheerful plant grows under trees in nature. It produces miniature tomato-like, but inedible, red fruits, which cover the bush. It enjoys fairly cool conditions.

Soil: Use commercial potting soil or a well-aerated mix of equal parts of garden loam, compost and river sand.

Light: Bright light.

Humidity: Average.

Watering: Water well, then allow the soil surface to dry out before watering again.

Feeding: Feed regularly with liquid food throughout the summer growing period.

Propagation: Seed or 10 cm tip cuttings.

Uses: The bright fruits of the solanum stand out well against their dark green leaves and help add colour to winter interiors. The solanum enjoys lots of fresh air and does well on cool windowsills.

Varieties: *S. pseudocapsicum,* the Jerusalem cherry, has orange-red berries. *S. pseudocapsicum* 'New Patterson', which is a dwarf and very compact variety, looks rather like a bonsai tree and is similar to, but more floriferous than the older but still popular 'Red Giant'. Another dwarf, *S. pseudocapsicum* 'Choker' has yellow berries which change to orange and through to red.

Stephanotis floribunda

Stephanotis floribunda
Madagascan jasmine

Habit: A twining creeper with stout stems and dense, dark green foliage, the stephanotis – often known as the bride's flower because its waxy, star-like tubular blooms are popular for bridal bouquets – makes a handsome plant. It produces quantities of fragrant flowers in summer.

Soil: Mix one third peat moss and some river sand with good commercial potting soil.

Light: Bright light and even a little sun in winter.

Humidity: Normal – about 25 per cent.

Watering: Water well, particularly in spring and summer, allowing the surface to dry to the touch before watering again. Always ensure that there is good drainage.

Feeding: Use liquid fertiliser fortnightly to encourage growth during spring and summer.

Propagation: Easiest by using 15 cm long tip cuttings which include about three leaves, or by seed.

Uses: Lovely subject for stoeps or near bright windows, preferably in a position where you will be able to enjoy its fragrance.

Streptocarpus hybrid

Streptocarpus hybrids
Cape primrose

Habit: The Cape primrose needs similar growing conditions to an African violet's. It is another of our indigenous plants that has been superbly hybridised overseas. The original plants all had blue or ivory-white flowers, but today colours include pink, lilac, purple and even red, and many have attractive markings in contrasting colours at the throat. The unusual funnel-like blooms grow on medium-length stems. They crowd posy-like at the centre of the plant, rising from the axils of long, oval leaves which arch over the edge of the container. These hybrids enjoy cool conditions.

Soil: A native of our tropical forests, the Cape primrose grows best in humus, but does very well in commercial potting soil or a mixture of half garden loam and half peat moss.

Light: Medium light is best for growth, followed by bright light for blooming, which can last from October through to late autumn.

Humidity: Raise from average in winter to high in summer. In dry inland areas a humidity tray is recommended.

Watering: Streptocarpuses need a lot of water during summer, but this should be reduced from May until the middle of August.

Feeding: Ensure that the soil is wet before feeding. Use a high-phosphate liquid fertiliser at half-strength fortnightly during summer.

Propagation: By seed, root division or by placing the edge of a leaf which has been cut across its width into soil at an oblique angle. Kept barely moist and in a medium light position, small plantlets will develop at the side of the cuttings within six weeks. These can then be separated and potted individually.

Uses: Streptocarpuses are neat, long-flowering plants that do very well on bright windowsills in kitchens and bathrooms where they appreciate the extra humidity. They are most attractive grouped together in hanging baskets.

Varieties: Many excellent named hybrids have been developed overseas, particularly in Germany, but they are very rarely sold by name in South Africa, colour preference appearing to be the deciding factor.

Thunbergia alata 'Lutea'

Thunbergia alata
Black-eyed Susan

Habit: Grown as an annual, this charming indigenous creeper is capable of covering quite a large area if given a trellis to grow on or allowed to trail from a basket. Pinch back regularly to encourage bushy growth. Its dainty flowers are orange and trumpet-shaped with dark throats and appear in great profusion under ideal circumstances.

Soil: Ordinary commercial potting soil is ideal, or use a friable mixture of equal parts good garden loam, compost and river sand.

Light: Very good light with some sun is needed. Will grow well in a sunny window but does best on a balcony or stoep.

Humidity: Average.

Watering: Must never dry out, but neither should it ever be soggy. Use the finger test regularly to check whether watering is necessary.

Feeding: Use liquid fertiliser fortnightly.

Propagation: Grow by seed in spring.

Uses: Thunbergias look attractive grown on a trellis, a wire column or trailing from a basket. This trailer always looks attractive planted with blue lobelia and white alyssum.

Varieties: *T. alata* 'Lutea' is similar with yellow flowers.

TIP: As old flowers die, they should be cut off. This encourages more blooms to take their place. Plant more than one in a bowl for a fuller effect.

2. Bulbs

Begonia tuberhybrida
Tuberous begonias

Habit: The flowers of tuberous begonias are surprisingly large and showy for the size of the plant. These blooms are like camellias in form, and up to 15 cm across. They are available in a wide range of colours – from white to soft pink, pale yellow, gold, salmon-pink, rose and red. Grown by tubers each spring, it is best to plant tuberous begonias singly in 15 cm pots. Tubers should be planted almost level with the soil surface.

Soil: Plant in a very porous soil mixture, including at least one third to half organic matter such as compost, plus some river sand.

Light: Bright light, such as on stoeps or near a bright north window. The new 'Non-stop' variety prefers a cooler southern window.

Humidity: Average.

Watering: Water well, but ensure that drainage is good, otherwise the tubers will rot. Allow the surface of the soil to start drying before watering again.

Feeding: Use the new, special slow-release 2:1:1(18) bulb food which has been created specifically for bulbs, or liquid food monthly.

Propagation: By tubers, seeds or cuttings.

Uses: Ideal pot plants for stoeps and bright, airy rooms.

Varieties: In addition to the camellia-type tuberous begonia, there is also a carnation-like variety and a very floriferous, pendulous type which is excellent for growing in hanging baskets. *B. tuberhybrida* 'Marginata' has dark edged petals. The best of these begonias is the new 'Non-stop' variety which flowers from October to April. This may be grown from seed.

Above: *Begonia tuberhybrida* 'Non-stop'
Below and right: *Begonia tuberhybrida* in various forms and colours

Freesia hybrids

Freesia hybrids

Habit: This lovely indigenous plant is now being developed for indoor use, providing trusses of bell-like, fragrant flowers on 30 cm tall wiry stems. Nurseries supply them in pots at the end of winter or early spring, but gardeners wishing to prepare their own should plant corms 7 cm apart, covered with 3 cm soil. Plant five corms in a 10 cm pot, seven in a 15 cm pot and 10 in a 20 cm pot.

Soil: Light, well-drained loam containing plenty of humus but no fresh manure. Freesias enjoy sandy soil.

Light: Pots should be placed outside where they receive full morning sun and light afternoon shade until the flower buds are fully formed, then bring them indoors. After flowering, place the plants in their pots in the garden until their leaves die back naturally.

Humidity: Freesias like fairly dry air.

Watering: From planting onwards, the soil in pots should never dry out completely, but should never be allowed to become waterlogged for long periods.

Feeding: Feed at the start of the flowering season with a special bulb food 2:1:1(18) and repeat monthly until the end of November.

Propagation: Stop watering in late November and place in a dry, dark spot at room temperature. Dig up corms in April, repot the large ones and plant the small ones in the garden.

Uses: Colourful and attractive, they make fine gifts and are a useful addition to the indoor scene, providing fragrance as well as beauty.

Varieties: Corms are available in separate colours: red, blue, yellow and white, or in a special golden variety, 'Golden Melody'.

TIP: Before the flower heads become heavy with blooms, tie the stems to small stakes. Plants showing signs of legginess should be given more light.

Hippeastrum varieties
Amaryllis

Habit: Hippeastrums produce one or two and sometimes three 30 cm tall stems topped by three to six huge trumpet-like blooms with a 20 cm diameter. Easy to grow and with attractive strap-like leaves, these plants put on a spectacular show for a long period and are a must for the home. Bulbs are large - 20-30 cm in circumference - and the bigger the bulb, the greater the chance of having more than one stem of flowers. Of all plants, the amaryllis produces the fastest results, flowering within five weeks of being potted. They are available in a wide range of colours and varieties from August until December.

Soil: Commercial potting soil or a mixture of equal parts of good garden loam, peat moss or compost, and river sand is ideal.

Light: Keep indoors in a bright position with a fairly constant temperature above 20 °C. Too little light produces tall, weak stems and leaves and poor blooms. Once stems start showing, rotate the pot 180 ° daily to prevent them from bending towards the light. After flowering, keep the plant growing in a sunny position until the end of summer to ensure good flowering the following season.

Humidity: Low.

Watering: Keep bulbs barely moist once planted and until the buds become visible. Once the buds are on the point of opening, increase the volume of water, but allow the surface soil to dry out before watering again. Once plants are in full growth, keep them constantly moist. After flowering, continue watering until mid-autumn, then place the pots on their sides so that you do not water them again until repotting them in spring.

Right, top to bottom: *Hippeastrum* varieties 'Milady', 'Bold Leader' and 'Barotse'
Below: *Hippeastrum* 'Blushing Bride'
Extreme right: *Hippeastrum* 'Safari'

Feeding: Start a feeding programme once the flowers have died to build the bulb up for flowering the following season. Use either an organic liquid food or the new special slow-release 2:1:1(18) bulb food now available. Old, well-rotted kraal manure may also be used. Hippeastrums are gross feeders.

Propagation: When repotting, remove small bulblets with as much root as possible from the base of the mother plant.

Uses: Whether presented singly, or potted in groups of three or five, hippeastrums make exciting indoor plants with flowers blooming over a long period. Groupings of single pots are also very effective, while many gardeners remove the plants from their pots just before flowering to include them in foliage plant arrangements.

TIP: Amaryllis prefer being snug in their pots, even if they do look out of proportion. A pot just a few centimetres wider than the bulb is all that is necessary. When planting, cover only about half of the bulb with soil, but ensure that the roots are spread out and firmly in place.

Hyacinthus varieties

Hyacinthus varieties
Hyacinth

Habit: Hyacinths are among the most fragrant of bulb flowers and have the added attraction of a lovely form – an upright spike with a mass of star-like mini-flowers crowding the top of the stem in bottlebrush style. They also offer a delightful range of soft pastel colours with a slightly frosted appearance – pale and dark blue, almost purple, pink, white and violet. When choosing hyacinths remember that the bigger the bulb, the bigger the flower. The heavy heads need some support, and this is best done by inserting thin wire through the flower stalk into the bulb.

Soil: Hyacinths prefer a fertile but well-drained soil and heavy soils should be made lighter with river sand. They grow well in commercial potting soil. They can also be grown without soil by placing them in a shallow dish among pebbles, with their bottoms barely touching the water. The modern, shaker-type bulb food can be sprinkled into the water.

Light: For indoor growing, force the bulb in a dark cupboard initially until about 5 cm of the bud has emerged from the bulb, then bring it into the light. Do not, however, place the pot in a position where it receives more than an hour's sunlight per day. Rotate the pot 180 ° every day or so to ensure that the stem grows straight and to prevent it from bending towards the light.

Humidity: Of no consequence.

Watering: Keep hyacinths constantly moist.

Feeding: Add the special bulb fertiliser 2:1:1(18) in powder form to the soil when planting, and once a month thereafter.

Propagation: Use offsets from the mother bulb.

Uses: Beautiful in single pots, or in bigger groups in bowls and even mixed with tulips and daffodils, they are a joy whichever way you use them.

TIP: An excellent way of educating children about plant growth is to have them grow a single hyacinth bulb in one of the special glass vases available. They can then see the roots develop from the bottom of the bulb as they seek the water below. The stem pushes upwards from the bulb at the same time, finally producing its glorious flowers. When using these vases, ensure that the bulb never rests in the water or it will rot – the roots will grow down to the water.

Lachenalia 'Roklara'

Lachenalia 'Ronette'

Lachenalia hybrids
Cape cowslip

Habit: Eleven new cultivars especially suited for use as indoor pot plants have recently been developed from hundreds of crossings of the original 79 species of these delightful veld flowers. Hybridised by the Roodeplaat Vegetable and Ornamental Research Institute especially for the South African pot plant market, they will become freely available to the general public in 1989. The eleven cultivars were chosen for their beautiful colours, their ability to produce many stems and a full effect in the pot, and their long flowering period. Some have fragrance as a bonus. Being bulbous plants, they produce fleshy spikes of tubular or bell-shaped blooms which densely drape more than half of their roughly 25 cm long stems. Some plants also have a hyacinth-like form. Colours range through varying shades of red, green, lilac, purple, blue and yellow, and many have attractive spotted or patterned leaves.

Soil: Lachenalias require a well-drained fertile soil – either commercial potting soil or one third good garden loam, one third compost and one third bark.

Light: Lachenalias grow in bright shade in nature, and do best in similar conditions indoors, without direct sun.

Humidity: Average, with day temperatures of 20-30 °C and night temperatures of 5-10 °C.

Watering: Plants should be kept moist but never wet.

Feeding: None necessary, provided soil is rich in organic material.

Propagation: Leaf cuttings.

Uses: Ideal as small colour plants for desk or table tops. They usually flower for six to eight weeks, about 10-16 weeks after planting in March or April. Lachenalias make ideal gifts.

Varieties: Some particularly attractive new hybrids are: *L.* 'Ronette' (yellow hyacinth-type with brown flecks), *L.* 'Robyn' (a red tubular variety), *L.* 'Roklara' (lilac), *L.* 'Romaud' (a fragrant yellow), and *L.* 'Rodelein' (a small purple hyacinth variety).

Leucojum aestivum
Snowflake

Habit: These attractive little plants are excellent substitutes for snowdrops (*Galanthus nivalis*) which are difficult to grow in most parts of South Africa. With lush foliage and charming, nodding little white bells with green-tipped petals, they make a delightful indoor plant.

Soil: Well-drained soil, with equal parts garden loam, peat moss and river sand.

Light: Bright light, even a little morning sun.

Humidity: Average.

Watering: Water regularly. Never allow them to dry out.

Feeding: Use special bulb food such as 2:1:1(18) when planting and only occasionally thereafter. Feed once with liquid fertiliser when they start flowering.

Propagation: By division, using small bulblets.

Uses: These dainty flowers are charming anywhere in the home where a small bowl of flowers is needed, from a narrow, south-facing windowsill to desk and table tops.

Leucojum aestivum

Lilium hybrids
Lilies

Habit: There are a great variety of lilies. Some are stately and discreet, others tall and colourful, and some are even scented. However, they all have one characteristic in common: they are stunningly beautiful, whether in the garden or grown in pots for indoor display. Flowers are generally trumpet-shaped, and the petals of some varieties, such as the Orientals, furl backwards. All have elegant, leafy stems topped by numerous blooms and need to be staked.

Soil: All need a well-aerated soil mix, including equal parts of garden soil, compost and river sand.

Light: Bright light near a sunny window with one or two hours of direct sunlight per day. Regularly rotate the pot 180° to prevent the plants from leaning towards the light source.

Humidity: Average.

Watering: Never allow the surface of the potting mixture to dry out. Keep constantly moist, but not waterlogged.

Feeding: Use special bulb food 2:1:1(18) in powder form when planting and a few more times before they flower, after which they should be given liquid food.

Propagation: By bulb scales.

Uses: Lilies grow tall and are very definitely for floor display, preferably in a place where the traffic will not disturb or damage the stems and flowers.

Varieties: There are a huge number of these, but the shorter varieties are best suited to indoor display.

Below and right, top to bottom: Four of the Orientals – 'Little Giant' (below), 'Connecticut King', 'Polka' and 'Shaka'

The always popular daffodil

Narcissus hybrids
Daffodil

Habit: This lovely genus of bulbs is greatly varied, but they all have basically the same requirements. The most popular types are the one-flower-to-a-stem trumpet daffodils, such as the common 'Flower Carpet', but there are also many attractive bicolours available. With the trumpet variety, the 'trumpet' is longer than each of the surrounding perianth (petal) segments, while with the cup variety, the 'cup' is stubbier and shorter than the surrounding perianth. All varieties have attractive, slender grass-like foliage.

Soil: Daffodils are excellent pot plants that grow in commercial potting soil or a mixture of equal quantities of good garden loam, peat moss or compost and river sand. Unlike most bulb varieties, daffodils grow vigorous roots and need pots at least 12,5 cm deep.

Light: As bright as possible.

Humidity: Average.

Watering: Keep moist, but the surface may dry out in between floodings.

Feeding: Use slow-release powder-type fertiliser 2:1:1(18) or organic liquid food once while flowering. Feed regularly until the leaves die down in order to build up bulbs for the following spring.

Propagation: By offsets around the mother plant.

Uses: Ideal for window boxes and all sorts of indoor containers. If you choose a container without holes, ensure that your bulbs are kept moist but not soggy. Daffodils in pots make charming gifts.

Varieties: In addition to the daffodils mentioned above, there is a great variety of others including double daffodils, such as 'Tahiti' (yellow frill with red inner petals), 'Unique' (white with yellow inner petals), and 'Acropolis' (white outer skirt with red and white inner petals), as well as Jonquil narcissuses which have a number of smaller, fragrant flowers to a stem. Others that are not commonly seen, and *Narcissus tazetta* varieties, are discussed separately in this chapter.

TIP: It is a good idea to plant double layers of daffodils in terracotta pots, with the top bulbs spaced in between those on the lower level. This creates a much fuller and more colourful effect.

Narcissus tazetta 'Paper White'

Narcissus tazetta 'Paper White'

Habit: This narcissus is particularly well suited to forcing indoors in pebbles. A lovely, dainty variety, it has a cluster of about eight small, white, fragrant blooms at the top of tall stems and is most attractive when massed in a bowl. Leaves are typically upright and grass-like as with other daffodil types.

Soil: Several different mediums may be used for forcing bulbs, but attractive small white river pebbles are the most popular and best suited to this variety. Special bulb fibre is difficult to find in South Africa, but another good growing medium is a mixture of peat moss and river sand.

Light: Some people start their bulbs in a dark cupboard, but this is not really necessary. They do very well started on the windowsill of a cool, sunless room (south-facing is ideal). It is most important that they should not be overheated, for while this may hasten growth, it eventually spoils them. If you start your bulbs in the dark, bring them out when the shoots are 3-4 cm high. Don't be alarmed at the anaemic yellow colour – this will soon turn green with improved light. Once growing, they may be gradually introduced to stronger light, but avoid direct sun. As they develop it is advisable to turn the bowl 180° from time to time. This will ensure an even growth pattern.

Humidity: Average.

Watering: This is the trickiest part of growing forced bulbs. Bulbs should be placed amongst the pebbles with their tips peeking out above the pebbles. The bowl should be filled with water so that it initially just touches the base of the bulbs to encourage root growth. Drop the water level thereafter to below the bulb to prevent bulb rot. Only the roots should rest in the water. The best method for checking the water level in relation to your bulbs is to stand a marked lollipop stick in the pebbles and remove it for examination. Add a few pieces of charcoal to the bottom of the bowl to keep the water sweet. If it should get smelly, take your bowl to the kitchen sink and flush it clean with a trickle of water. Remove excess water with a syphon.

Feeding: Dilute liquid fertiliser and feed occasionally while growing.

Propagation: By offsets around the mother plant.

Uses: Forced bulbs in attractive bowls – the Chinese style is very suitable – are most decorative and a wonderful reminder of the coming of spring.

TIP: Bigger bulbs give bigger flower heads, but for a more massed flower effect it is better to use a greater number of smaller bulbs which should barely touch one another in the bowl. When buying your bulbs, ensure that they are firm and unscarred.

The classic-looking tulip

Tulip hybrids

Habit: The genus *Tulipa* is a vast one, with a tremendous colour and form range. It has been developed from a few hundred varieties known in the 17th century to 4 000 odd today. Of these, about 800 varieties are grown commercially, but in South Africa we stick mainly to the classic Darwin hybrids. Amongst the biggest of the tulips, this easy-to-grow strain has perfectly shaped blooms on tall, strong stems and abundant bluish-green foliage.

Soil: It is most important that their soil be well drained, with lots of humus and river sand included in the mix. Equal quantities of each is about right.

Light: As bright as possible. They are best grown out of doors in South Africa, then brought into the home in bud.

Humidity: Average.

Watering: Keep soil moist, never allowing it to dry out.

Feeding: Use special slow-release bulb food 2:1:1(18) when planting, and then liquid food once during their flowering spell.

Propagation: Use offsets attached to the parent bulb.

Uses: Nothing brings spring into the home the way a bowl of tulips does. Wonderful for decoration virtually anywhere in the house, a pot of tulips also makes an exciting gift.

Varieties: *T.* 'Apeldoorn', a brilliant vermilion red tulip, is the most cultivated tulip variety in the world and certainly the most popular in South Africa. Other tulips in South Africa are generally sold by colour rather than name and those available include white, a variety of pinks, orange, yellow and red.

3. Bromeliads

Aechmea fasciata

Aechmea varieties
Urn plant

Habit: The most widely cultivated of bromeliads, aechmeas are not only showy but are amongst the easiest to grow. They have striking, sturdy foliage, often vividly coloured and arranged in graceful, tubular open rosettes. Spiny-edged leaves may be soft or rigid, glossy or covered with scales and either coloured green, rose, maroon or even a purple-brown, and may be barred, striped, mottled or have a combination of all three. Flowers are borne on tall, leafless stems rising from the centre of plants and may be globular, pendulous, cylindrical or erect. Many aechmea varieties have colourful long-lasting bracts and all produce charming, berry-like fruits – often their chief attraction.

Soil: When grown in pots, use a porous mixture: coarse washed river sand or pebbles, chopped pine bark in various sizes, with a little wood charcoal to keep the soil sweet.

Light: Bright light or about 50 per cent shade for *A. chantinii, A. fasciata, A. orlandiana*, but less light for those having softer leaves, such as *A.* 'Foster's Favorite', *A. fulgens* 'Discolor', *A.* 'Red Ribbon' and *A.* 'Royal Wine'.

Humidity: Average – they thrive in Natal coastal conditions. Mist regularly indoors in less humid areas.

Watering: The natural vase in the centre of the plant should always be kept filled with water, but the soil surface may be allowed to dry out somewhat between waterings.

Feeding: In nature they make their own 'liquid manure' in their vase – a natural water storage tank – but if kept indoors it is wise to feed them fortnightly with a well-balanced organic liquid foliar feed.

Propagation: Offsets form naturally at the base of the plant and may be removed easily when they've reached more than a third of their mature size for aechmeas have very small root systems.

Uses: Ideal for display in pots, on large pieces of driftwood or on bromeliad trees in indoor gardens.

Varieties: A long-lasting house plant, *A. fasciata* has broad, silver-dusted leaves and frosted pink bracts with violet-blue petals. *A. chantinii* has silver-banded green to black-green leaves and striking orange-red, ribbon-like bracts with bright yellow and red petals. A feature of *A. fulgens* 'Discolor' is its rose-red berries, tipped with purple flowers, and glossy, leathery leaves, which are green on top and purple underneath. *A. orlandiana* has zebra-like, brown-banded, glossy green leaves and yellow flowers with persistent scarlet bracts. Attractive new varieties are: *A.* 'Foster's Favorite' with lacquered, wine-red, strap-like leaves and a pendulous spike of coral-petalled flowers tipped with blue; *A.* 'Red Ribbon' has a red stripe in the centre of informal, arching leaves and a pendulous flower/berry inflorescence; and *A.* 'Royal Wine' has glossy green and maroon leaves with spikes of orange berries.

TIP: Bromeliads look stunning displayed on a bromeliad tree made from driftwood or old tree stumps found in the veld. Choose a shallow bowl and into this 'plant' your tree. Fill in around the base with heavy stones to hold the trunk, before setting it in plaster of Paris. When doing this, form several basins in the surface of the plaster. Once it's set, plant some of the bigger bromeliad varieties into these cavities and attach various bromeliads in the crooks between branches or even against the tree. Drape or hang some of the lighter, smaller airplants (*Tillandsia* varieties) on the thinner stems.

Cover the base of each bromeliad with damp sphagnum moss. Then attach it either to some porous material such as slabs of bark or cork and then to the tree, or directly to the tree with thin, plastic coated wire. Always ensure that vase type bromeliads are level so that their vases may be kept filled with water. Airplants may be stapled or gummed with model aeroplane glue directly to stems.

Ananas bracteatus
Pineapple plant

Habit: A terrestrial bromeliad which produces startling, large, pineapple-like fruit, while the plant has outstandingly decorative but spiny, broad leaves.

Soil: Needs a fertile yet open, gritty soil which includes quantities of washed river sand and leaf mould.

Light: Full sun to 50 per cent shade.

Humidity: Above 25 per cent.

Watering: Allow the surface soil to dry out between waterings.

Feeding: Feed every two months with good organic liquid fertiliser.

Propagation: From leaf rosettes formed at the top of the fruit, or from plantlets growing at the base of the plant.

Uses: Ideal for brightening indoor gardens and mixed arrangements, such as in flat bowls or at the base of bromeliad trees.

Varieties: *A. bracteatus* has arching, spiny, bronze-red leaves and pink-red, edible, acid pineapple-like fruit. *A. bracteatus* 'Striatus' is a medium-to-large plant with pink-tinged, broad cream and green striped leaves. It produces scarlet 'pineapples'. *A. comosus* 'Variegatus' is a decorative indoor form of the pineapple, *A. comosus*, and has cream and green leaves.

Below: *Ananas bracteatus* 'Striatus'
Bottom: *Ananas comosus* 'Variegatus'

Billbergia varieties
Fishpole plants

Habit: As with the entire bromeliad family, these small-rooted plants have perfect vase forms for collecting water and food and are ideal house plants. They are far easier and faster to grow than most people would imagine, and are almost indestructible. With a charming shape and foliage, billbergias produce spectacular, if short-lived flower spikes in summer and make ideal centrepieces for indoor arrangements.

Soil: Being epiphytes, their roots really only need something to hold to, such as pebbles and pieces of bark in equal proportions, as they don't absorb much water or many nutrients.

Light: Medium to bright for best foliage colour, but will tolerate very low-light conditions, making them a valuable indoor plant.

Humidity: Above average – billbergias appreciate misting.

Watering: Keep the vase filled, preferably with rainwater, and wet the potting medium at regular intervals.

Feeding: Foliar feed monthly. Overfeeding promotes a too lush growth.

Propagation: By means of offsets when semi-mature.

Uses: Brightly coloured billbergias are ideal for modern décor schemes and look particularly good in glazed bowls.

Cryptanthus hybrids
Earth stars

Habit: Easy to cultivate, these terrestrial plants, rarely larger than 25 cm in diameter, have leaves which are more crinkly than those of other bromeliads. These are generally mottled or striped with brown, rose, green, silver, chartreuse, grey or copper. Dainty little white flowers emerge from the centres of their rosettes of leaves.

Soil: Generally found growing in well-drained, humus-rich soil in nature, cryptanthuses are best cultivated in a mixture containing quantities of organic matter plus gritty river sand for drainage.

Light: This will vary from bright sunlight to medium light, depending on the particular variety. In their native Brazil they generally grow on the forest floor, with some receiving more shade than others. Check with your nurseryman which light conditions your plant favours. *C. acaulis* and *C. bivittatus*, for example, need about 70 per cent shade, while *C. bromelioides tricolor* prefers only about 40 per cent shade and *C.* 'Carnival de Rio' even deeper shade for best colouring.

Humidity: High humidity, making them ideal terrarium plants.

Watering: Soil should always be damp, as cryptanthuses have no vase or water reservoir to tide them over.

Billbergia variety

Billbergia pyramidalis 'Concolour'

They are also attractive grown on wood stumps or driftwood in indoor gardens.

Varieties: *B.* 'Fantasia' is a show stopper with handsome, cream-spotted leaves and bright red bracts with violet-red petals. *B. nutans* (queen's tears), with narrow, olive green leaves which turn red in bright sunlight, produces bright pink, pendulous bracts with nodding, green, violet-edged flowers. *B. pyramidalis* 'Concolour' has short-lived but spectacular pink flowers.

Feeding: Use normal strength liquid food every two months.

Propagation: Use offsets which develop between the leaves and at the base of the plant when a third the size of the mature plant.

Uses: Ideal for terrariums, containers, pebble dish gardens and for growing in soil at the base of bromeliad trees. Some are suitable for hanging bowls. Extremely decorative when well grown and deserve to be better known and used. The many hundreds of hybrids now available are so attractive that they are certain to become very popular with indoor gardeners.

Varieties: There are new varieties coming onto the market all the time, but the following are particularly worthwhile: *C. bivittatus* 'Minor' has small rosettes of brown-pink leaves with bands of silver-green. *C.* 'Cafe au Lait', another mini-variety, has compact, small rosettes with pink and tan wavy-edged leaves. *C. bivittatus* 'Pink Starlite' has bright pink, green and white striped leaves and needs strong light. *C. bivittatus* 'Major' is a larger, lush variety with brown-pink leaves and silver-green stripes. *C. bivittatus* 'Ruby Red' is a new dwarf cultivar with ruby-red colouring and darker stripes. *C.* 'Carnival de Rio' has arching, olive-green leaves with mottled red-pink tints. *C.* 'Candy Apple' is a compact, multicoloured variety blotched with shades of pink, brown and green. *C. zonatus* 'Fudge Ripple' has a large, lush rosette with colourful, snake-like leaves. *C.* 'Red Waves' is large and robust with silvery-maroon foliage. *C.* 'It' has a large, leathery rosette with a spectacular pink margin and stripes on a green background. *C.* '3i' has reverse markings to *C.* 'It' which are even more startling.

Cryptanthus bivittatus 'Major'

Guzmania varieties

Habit: Winter and spring flowering guzmanias are mainly epiphytic but grow more luxuriantly when cultivated as conventional pot plants. They have smooth-edged, glossy leaves, often with vertical maroon lines. Their upright and long-lasting inflorescences have brilliantly coloured red, yellow and orange bracts with white or yellow flowers.

Soil: Provide with an open, gritty soil medium which includes composted pine bark and a little charcoal.

Light: Medium to bright but never less than 50 per cent shade.

Humidity: Coming mainly from the Andean rain forests, guzmanias prefer a high humidity. They need to be misted or washed down regularly to last well indoors.

Watering: Guzmanias enjoy being moist and their vases should be filled with water at all times.

Feeding: Liquid fertiliser every two months.

Propagation: By offsets from the base of the parent plant once plantlets are a third or more the size of the mature plant.

Uses: Decorative in containers and plant groupings, but they don't thrive on bromeliad trees as they need more sheltered growing conditions.

Varieties: *G. lingulata* 'Cardinalis' has a medium-large, open rosette of lush lettuce-green leaves, a spectacular inflorescence of scarlet bracts and white flowers high above its foliage. *G. lingulata* 'Minor Orange' or 'Minor Red' has small compact rosettes of bronze-red leaves, bright scarlet bracts and white flowers set low in the centre, and *G. lingulata* 'Major' has long-lasting orange bracts. *G. musaica* has bizarre, snake-like markings with striking crossbands and an orange inflorescence. *G.* 'Zahnii' has a fairly large rosette of richly coloured, copper-red leaves and a stout lemon-yellow inflorescence (prefers low-light conditions). *G.* 'Amaranth' has green, strap-like leaves and a tall showy amaranth inflorescence. *G.* 'Empire' has a compact bronze-red or green rosette with cherry-red bracts. *G.* 'Grand Prix' has long, green, strap-like leaves and crimson recurving bracts on tall stems. *G.* 'Mini Exodus' has a medium-large rosette, glossy maroon leaves and lighter maroon bracts.

Guzmania lingulata 'Major'

Neoregelia 'Victoria-pedilla'

Neoregelia varieties
Blushing bromeliad

Habit: Growing mainly on the ground and lower branches of trees, these epiphytic shade-lovers are compact, medium-sized members of the bromeliad group with leathery, glossy leaves which may be plain or silvery-green, maroon, banded, spotted, striped or marbled. Flowers of neoregelias nestle in a compound head in the heart of the plant. During flowering in late spring and summer the centre leaves of many neoregelias turn to shades of bright red, pink and purple. Neoregelias are ideal for cooler areas of the country as they are able to withstand low temperatures.

Soil: Neoregelias grow well in any gritty, well-drained medium but prefer a mixture of chopped bark and washed river pebbles, with a little leaf mould or well-rotted compost.

Light: Medium to bright light. The shadier the area, the longer and greener the leaves. Under brighter conditions, the leaves tend to be brighter, shaded red and purple and the plants flower better. Fifty per cent shade is ideal.

Humidity: Medium, but if the leaf edges turn brown, increase the humidity slightly.

Watering: Ensure that the dam at the centre of the rosette formed by the leaves is always filled with water.

Neoregelia carolinae 'Tricolor'

Feeding: Liquid food monthly.

Propagation: By offsets found at the base of the parent plant when a third or more of the mature size.

Uses: Neoregelias are highly decorative, and suitable for dish arrangements and bromeliad trees.

Varieties: *N. carolinae*, one of the showiest and most popular varieties, has shiny, green leaves with a fiery red centre. *N. carolinae* 'Tricolor' is equally popular, especially as a pot plant. Its leaves are striped in ivory, green and rose. *N. chlorosticta* has firm, colourful leaves varying from olive green to mottled plum. *N. schultesiana* 'Fireball' has a startling small flat compact rosette of brilliant red leaves, becoming even more luminous when producing its blue flowers. It spreads rapidly to form a colony. *N. spectabilis* (painted fingernail plant) has arching, olive-green leaves with brilliant red tips. 'Meyendorfii' is a chubbier looking form of *N. carolinae* and is a selected cultivar which has been commercialised. *N.* 'Flandria' has particularly bright, variegated leaves and a good form. *N.* 'Morris Henry Hobbs' is a spectacular, tough, maroon-leafed rosette with a good form. *N.* 'Ampullacea' has stoloniferous dwarf rosettes that quickly form colonies with a bizarre form and appearance, and comes in many varieties, shapes, sizes and colours. *N.* 'Decora' has large, thick-set rosettes of glossy, leathery leaves which have spectacular, violet-lavender centre leaves and *N.* 'Victoria-pedilla' has striking amethyst inner bracts.

Nidularium varieties

Friendship plant; blushing cup

Habit: Nidulariums grow in dark, humid forests, generally among rotted debris on the ground or on low branches. These members of the Bromeliaceae form medium-sized, flat rosettes of firm, glossy leaves, varying in colour from green to dark purple. They are sometimes soft but always have toothed edges. A collarette of short leaves in the heart of the plant turns brilliant rose, cerise, red, white or blue shortly before producing its flowers which mound compactly in the water of the vase that they form.

Soil: Use a gritty, open soil mix, including peat moss or compost and river sand, or 50 per cent peat moss and 50 per cent chopped pine bark.

Light: Nidulariums will survive in very low light, but have a much better form and colour when grown in better light with 60-70 per cent shade.

Humidity: Nidulariums enjoy both high humidity and high temperatures but can survive dryness and some cold with fortitude.

Watering: Keep moist and ensure that the central rosette is always filled with water.

Feeding: Nidulariums respond well to a monthly feeding with regular-strength organic liquid fertiliser.

Propagation: From offsets formed at the base of the plant when approximately a third of the mature plant's size.

Uses: Decorative, and suitable for indoor dish or container arrangements, and for growing on driftwood.

Varieties: *N. innocentii* 'Innocentii' is a truly beautiful bromeliad with a medium-sized rosette of soft, metallic purple leaves, and a rusty-red inner rosette of white flowers. *N. innocentii lineatum* and *N. innocentii striatum* are similar to the previous variety except that their leaves are fresh lettuce-green striped snow-white and creamy-yellow respectively. *N. regelioides* has compact, shiny green leaves with darker mottling, and a rose-coloured inner rosette that becomes red with age. *N. billbergioides*, an ideal ground cover, has soft, green leaves glowing with burnt orange or sulphur yellow flower bracts. *N. fulgens* has a tough, symmetrical rosette of glossy green, blotched leaves and contrasting orange-red flower bracts. *N.* 'Casmir Morobe' has a large, glossy green rosette with striking crimson bracts. *N.* 'Rutilans' has dark green, patterned leaves and incredible lilac central bracts.

Nidularium innocentii

Tillandsia brachycavlos

Tillandsia flabellata

Tillandsia varieties
Air plants

Habit: The common name of these remarkable epiphytic plants is very apt for they appear to live on little but air. They do, however, need moisture and food. Their extremely small root system is in most cases used only to cling to a host. Forms vary from the lichen-like Spanish moss to large grey, scaly, octupus-like desert species, and soft green leaf varieties found in humid forests. Some merely form rosettes of spindly leaves. An added attraction of most tillandsias is their fascinating, usually lance-like flowers, which may last for some months.

Soil: Most varieties, such as Spanish moss, which in nature cling to the branches of trees, need no soil. Some may be pinned to supports (driftwood, corkbark or cactus skeletons) while others, such as *T. cyanea*, which grows and looks more like a normal bromeliad, need a quick-draining mixture made up of such items as finely chopped bark, sphagnum moss and perlite or vermiculite in equal proportions, but no soil. All tillandsias need free air movement and hate stuffy rooms.

Light: Varieties vary in their light requirements. Some need medium light, while others require direct sun, but most need bright, dappled light. Sunlight is their most important cultural requirement and the plants tell you what they need. Those with stiff leaves or leaves which are grey-white in colour usually come from deserts and like the most sunlight, while those with greener, softer leaves come from rain forests and prefer less light.

Humidity: Average to high.

Watering: Rooting varieties should be kept slightly moist, while most of the rootless ones, with the exception of the desert species, should do well misted or dunked in water once or twice a week, and daily in summer. The scalier the plant, the less water it needs. Household tillandsias should be put out in the rain whenever possible.

Feeding: Occasional weak solutions of organic liquid fertiliser applied in a misty spray form are best as tillandsias absorb nutriments through the scales on their leaves.

Propagation: Generally by way of foliar offsets, known as pups, when about one third the size of the parent plant.

Uses: They are excellent for artificial light gardens and should be grown about 30 cm from the light source above a humidity tray containing moisture to ensure humidity. They also make excellent additions to bromeliad trees.

Varieties: There are over 400 varieties, making tillandsias the biggest genus of any Bromeliaceae. Some attractive and generally available forms are: *T. cyanea*, which forms small, grass-like, green rosettes with a fan-shaped bright rose inflorescence and blue flowers; *T. ionantha*, normally grey-green in colour, turning bright red when it flowers in summer; *T. atroviridipetala*, a small variety with grey-green leaves and pinky-red blooms, which is used to dry conditions; *T. stricta*, which has thin leaves with silvery scales forming a compact rosette from which appear rose-coloured bracts with violet-blue petals; *T. brachycavlos* which has red bracts and violet flowers; *T. flabellata*, a candelabrum variety with scarlet bracts and blue-violet flowers and *T. usneoides* (Spanish moss), which produces colonies of long thread-like strands. Others, used strictly for mounting, are: *T. aeranthos* with red bracts and purple petals; *T. ixioides* with bright yellow petals; *T. araujei* with pink and white petalled flowers; and *T. juncea* with red bracts and bluish-purple petals.

Vriesea varieties

Flaming sword

Habit: Like all bromeliads, vrieseas enjoy a buoyant atmosphere with a lot of air movement, but no strong wind. Mainly epiphytic, they vary in size from miniatures to 2 m tall, but most home varieties are compact, with smooth-edged leaves varying in colour from a bright, light green to bronze-maroon. Most often plain green, some are also barred or spotted. The inflorescence usually bears a tall, flattened, lance-shaped spike, with long-lasting purple, red, yellow or green bracts and yellow, white or green flowers.

Soil: Your growing medium should comprise equal parts chopped bark and river pebbles or grit, as most of the popular varieties available are epiphytic and don't grow in soil.

Light: Bright dappled light and 60 per cent shade.

Humidity: Medium to high as it encourages growth.

Watering: Keep the vase filled with water at all times, though the planting medium may dry out a little without causing problems.

Feeding: Organic liquid food as a foliar spray monthly.

Propagation: Separate plantlets from the base of the parent plant.

Vriesea perfecta

Vriesea 'Favourite' (front) and *Vriesea* 'Flammea-Duval' hybrid (back)

Uses: One of the most popular of the bromeliad species because of its decorative value and long-lasting floral bracts.

Varieties: Literally hundreds of colourful new hybrids are becoming available, but here are some of the best old varieties, plus some of the new: *V. carinata* has a flattened spike with crimson bracts and bright yellow flowers which appear from a small rosette of lettuce-green leaves; the popular painted feather or *V. mariae* has a compact, medium-sized rosette of light, lettuce-green leaves and a tall spike with a flattened inflorescence consisting of glowing red bracts tipped with yellow, as well as yellow flowers; *V. splendens* or flaming sword has copper-brown, barred leaves and a bonus of a brilliant red 'sword'; *V. perfecta* is a candelabrum variety with flaming red bracts; *V. rex* has a regal yellow and dark red flower stalk rising from a symmetrical green-tinged maroon rosette of leaves; *V.* 'Poelmanii' is a strikingly handsome plant with a glowing candelabrum flower spike with red bracts; *V.* 'Gloriosa' is a small, compact rosette with free-flowering red fish-like flowers; *V.* 'Rubin' is a small, cute rosette with almost too-large bright red flower bracts; *V.* 'Vulcan' is a sturdy, compact plant with a long-lasting candelabrum with red bracts; *V.* 'Fulgida' is an easy-to-grow green rosette with orange-red, feathery flowers; *V.* 'Favourite' has long-lasting, elegant red bracts; and *V.* 'Flammea-Duval' is a showy candelabrum variety with red bracts.

4. Foliage plants

Aglaonema varieties

Habit: Aglaonemas are close relations of the arum lily, but have less exciting flowers. They are probably the most rewarding, tough, no-nonsense yet attractive foliage plants in the world, and capable of surviving in the dimmest positions. Leaves are generally lance-shaped with varieties varying in colour from light to blue-green and dark green and yellow to silver, and are generally streaked with different greens.

Soil: Aglaonemas require a rather special soil of equal parts of good garden loam, peat moss and river sand. If you wish, you may also include some bark. To each bucket of your mixture add one-and-a-half teaspoonfuls of superphosphate, one tablespoon limestone and two teaspoonfuls of 2:3:2 fertiliser.

Light: Low to medium; plants become somewhat spindly if given too much light. Successful even with only eight hours of artificial light in office situations.

Humidity: Medium.

Watering: Keep barely moist at all times and a little drier in winter. Ensure that no water is left in the saucer.

Feeding: Either a good feed with organic liquid fertiliser quarterly or a weak solution fortnightly.

Propagation: Stem and tip cuttings as well as by division of offsets forming at the base of the mother plant.

Uses: Suitable for practically any position in the house, this is one plant variety that no home should be without. It is particularly useful for brightening corners where few other plants would grow. Offering a variety of sizes and foliage colours, miniatures look great on coffee tables, while the others look effective in containers on the floor. Several of the same variety grouped together in a 25 cm pot create the most impact.

Varieties: *A. commutatum* has soft green leaves with silver streaks, and reaches a height of 60 cm. *A. commutatum* 'Pseudobracteatum' is a taller-growing dieffenbachia-like

Aglaonema crispum 'Silver Queen'

variety (50-65 cm tall) with variegated green and yellow leaves. *A. commutatum* 'Maria' is a new low-growing, very bushy and compact variety having dark green leaves with darker green flecks. *A. commutatum* 'Abidjane' is another new form with broader than usual leaves which grow to about 75 cm. Also bushy, its leaves are blue-green with darker flecks. *A. crispum* 'Silver Queen' is a very compact plant with striking, silvery leaves, which are narrower than those of most aglaonemas. *A. commutatum* 'Silver Spear' is similar in colour to *A. crispum* 'Silver Queen' and also very compact, but with even narrower leaves. They are an excellent choice for lightening dark corners.

TIP: Prune your aglaonemas back when they become too large and use tip cuttings to propagate more plants. These may be rooted in water and make excellent foliage vase decorations until ready for planting.

Aglaonema commutatum 'Pseudobracteatum'

Aglaonema commutatum 'Silver Spear'

Asparagus densiflorus 'Meyerii'

Asparagus setaceus

Asparagus varieties
Asparagus ferns

Habit: This large species of plants, a number of which are native to South Africa, are well suited to growing indoors, provided they are kept in light positions. They all have extremely attractive foliage and there are both upright and trailing varieties. Although often referred to as ferns because of their soft and attractive appearance, they are not in fact ferns at all, but related to the asparagus vegetable and are part of the lily family.

Soil: Asparagus ferns need a very light, well-aerated soil mix – the commercial varieties are most suitable – otherwise add equal parts of organic matter and some river sand to your normal soil.

Light: All asparagus ferns need good light and thrive in north-facing rooms with filter curtains. *A. setaceus* can take dimmer light than the rest, and *A. densiflorus* 'Sprengeri' does well in bathrooms and is able to take a little more humidity than others.

Humidity: Average, but increase the humidity if you notice leaf drop.

Watering: Plants should have ample water during their growing period and should not be allowed to dry out. Watering should be reduced during cooler months.

Feeding: Use liquid food monthly for most of the year but stop during winter.

Propagation: Division of roots in spring is easiest, but also by seed.

Uses: Depending on whether they are upright or trailing, asparagus ferns look very attractive in pots or hanging baskets.

Varieties: *A. setaceus* (*A. plumosus* 'Nana') is a lovely feathery plant with extremely fine, lacy, dark green, soft foliage; *A. densiflorus* 'Meyerii' is often known as the cat's tail asparagus due to its upright, tail-like fronds and *A. falcatus* is an upright variety with rather coarser leaves, which enjoys warmer conditions than the others. The beautiful trailing variety *A. densiflorus* 'Sprengeri' produces honey-scented, little white flowers which later turn into attractive red berries under ideal conditions.

Aspidistra elatior
Cast-iron plant

Habit: Unfussy and tough, this remarkable plant deserves its common name on account of its nature, but the name bears no relation to its appearance. With softly arching, broad, dark green leaves rising from a rhizome to a height of 90 cm, it is far more handsome than the name suggests. It is not surprising that this striking plant, which forms a fountain of foliage, was one of the most popular plants for dark parlours in Victorian times.

Soil: Equal parts of garden loam, peat moss and river sand, plus two teaspoonfuls of superphosphate, two teaspoonfuls SR3:2:1(28) general fertiliser and four teaspoonfuls ground limestone added to a bucket of the mixture.

Light: An ideal plant for a south-facing window, but may take even dimmer light.

Humidity: Low.

Watering: Keep barely moist. Although it will live under drought conditions, it does not enjoy them.

Feeding: Little feeding is necessary if the original soil is properly structured, but you may feed with a little organic liquid fertiliser during the summer growing period. Overfeeding will cause the leaves to split.

Propagation: Slow-growing aspidistras should be divided and repotted only very occasionally, certainly no more than every five years. In spring, divide the roots, taking a few leaves with each piece of root. To encourage a fine, healthy and bushy plant, place several such roots in a pot.

Uses: The aspidistra should never have lost its Victorian popularity, for it is still one of the best indoor plants where something substantial is required in a rather dim situation. In a brass pot and with its leaves kept shiny clean, it is most attractive.

Varieties: *A. elatior* 'Variegata' is similar to the green variety but has bands of cream in its leaves. Not quite as hardy as the green variety.

Aspidistra elatior

Beaucarnea nolina (left) and *Beaucarnea recurvata* (right)

Beaucarnea recurvata
Elephant's foot plant

Habit: Also known as a bottle palm because of its bottle shape when small, this fine accent plant has a broad stem ending in a point like an onion, with long leaves cascading like a mop from its tip. As the water-storing base develops and gets broader, so the texture of the trunk becomes rougher and like elephant hide, while the foliage becomes more dense.

Soil: Needs a well-drained soil with a lot of compost and river sand mixed with potting soil to ensure good drainage.

Light: Should have good light, even some sun if possible.

Humidity: Low.

Watering: Coming from Mexican desert areas, this plant has a bulbous base holding water. Care must be taken not to overwater and cause root rot. It is best to water it thoroughly and to then leave it to dry out before watering again.

Feeding: Liquid food every two months.

Propagation: By seed.

Uses: This is certainly a plant you cannot ignore. It is very much a decorator's plant because of its rather weird but dramatic appearance. It is very useful where a strong focal point is needed in a room. Although it rarely grows more than a metre high indoors, it has very bold, distinctive outlines and is best appreciated in uncluttered surroundings.

Varieties: *Beaucarnea nolina* has similar foliage on a taller stem and is easier to grow, but its onion-shaped base does not develop as large and distinctive a stem as *B. recurvata*, which retains its bottle-like appearance.

> **TIP:** Should the central leaves lose colour and turn pale green, place the plant in the sun and it will quickly regain its original colour.

Begonia **foliage varieties**

Habit: There are several begonia types, but the tender, fleshy and non-woody foliage begonias discussed here have striking, intricately patterned leaves, some hairy, others not.

The rex begonias are the most colourful members of this fascinating and varied group. They have slightly elongated, heart-shaped leaves with bright splashes of orange and red, brown and lilac, yellow and green, and pink and silver. Each large leaf is supported by a stem about 30 cm long, rising directly from the rhizome to form large clumps. The growth pattern is very similar to *B. boweri*, *B. masoniana* and *B.* 'Cleopatra'.

Soil: Provide a well-aerated mixture made up of equal parts of good potting soil, compost and river sand.

Light: Very bright light with some sunlight ensures good growth and bold-coloured leaves.

Humidity: Enjoying high humidity, they do best in subtropical conditions and thrive along the Natal coast. They also do well in South Africa's dry heartland, particularly if provided with humidity trays half-filled with water.

Watering: Rex begonias grow naturally on forest floors and along the banks of streams and in other moist places, and must therefore not be allowed to dry out in pots except during winter when the soil surface may be allowed to dry slightly. At all other times keep moist but not wet.

Feeding: Fertilise regularly every two weeks with good liquid food throughout the warm months when growth is at its peak.

Propagation: This may be done either by division at repotting stage or by 10 cm-long tip and leaf cuttings during spring and early summer. Dipped in a hormone powder and placed in a peat moss and river sand mixture, these take about six weeks to root.

Uses: An excellent choice for light positions in the home and for brightening up plant arrangements.

Varieties: One of the brightest rex begonias is 'Merry Christmas', with splashes of silver and orange, pink, lilac, red and green, but others of note are 'Yuletide' and 'Silver Queen'. The range of colour blends is quite amazing. *Begonia masoniana* 'Iron Cross' is another most attractive variety with rough-textured, green leaves bearing a dark brown cross as decoration. *B.* 'Cleopatra' has soft looking, downy green and brown leaves. The green leaves of *B. boweri* are edged with brown or black and as a bonus it has charming small white and pink flowers. *B.* 'Black Beauty' is a dark, velvety green stunner.

Below, left and right: *Begonia rex* varieties

Caladium hortulanum varieties

Habit: A plant for the warm months of the year, this spectacularly beautiful tropical swamp lover thrives in warm, humid places from spring until autumn. With large, often 30 cm long, heart-shaped leaves, it provides bright splashes of colour that few other plants can match. Translucent, parchment thin leaves rise from the pot on long stalks.

Soil: Use leaf mould, garden loam and river sand in proportions of 3, 2 and 1 respectively.

Light: As bright as possible, without direct sunlight. They burn rapidly if the sun shines on them through glass.

Temperature: Warmth is vital for these plants, the ideal temperature being about 25 °C, but it should never be below 18 °C, even during autumn and winter.

Humidity: This should be high. In dry inland areas place them on a humidity tray and mist the leaves daily.

Watering: Caladiums are one of the few indoor plants that can survive overwatering, for in nature these beauties normally grow along the banks of streams or swamps. They need a lot of moisture during the warm growing months, but reduce watering as winter approaches.

Feeding: Use liquid manure fortnightly.

Propagation: Remove small offsets from the main tuber when leaves start sprouting.

Uses: Admirable plants for providing colour in summer and for arrangements where separate pots are used. Do not, however, include in densely planted arrangements, for they enjoy more water than most other indoor plants.

Varieties: There are a great many hybrids but it is difficult to buy them by name – one needs to see the colours. There are many marbled mixtures such as white with bright green veins (*C. hortulanum* 'Candidum'); green or white with red veins (*C. hortulanum* 'Angel's Wings'); pink with green veins (*C. hortulanum* 'Lord Derby'); translucent pink with dark pink veins (*C. hortulanum* 'Gypsy Rose'); mottled green with a pinky-red centre (*C. hortulanum* 'Rosebud'); red veins and a plain red centre with green edging (*C. hortulanum* 'Mrs Hemple') and many, many more.

Caladium hortulanum 'Lord Derby' (red) and 'Gypsy Rose'

TIP: As summer passes, caladium leaves slowly die down. At this stage you should start reducing watering and turn the pot on its side so that you are not tempted to water again until spring. Begin watering again in about September. The best time to divide plantlets from the mother tuber is when the leaves start to sprout. When separating, be careful not to damage the new roots. Use the smallest container possible when repotting. Only tubers of the same size should be planted in the same pot. Plant the entire tuber 3 cm beneath the surface of the soil.

Below, left to right: A variety of *Caladium hortulanum* hybrids

Calathea picturata 'Argentea'

Calathea zebrina

Calathea varieties
Peacock plants

Habit: More upright than its close relative the maranta; the colourful feather-like patterns on the leaves of this genus makes the choice of its common name obvious. It has rather specific demands which make it one of the more difficult of indoor plants to grow, but its attractive appearance certainly makes it worth the extra trouble. It cannot take sun, draughts or dry conditions. The following plant requirement pointers need to be adhered to strictly.

Soil: In nature calatheas grow in the compost of South American forest floors and accordingly need a rich, light soil of equal parts of peat moss, vermiculite or perlite and river sand, plus a half part of well-rotted and sieved kraal manure.

Light: Calatheas prefer dappled light, and do well behind a filter curtain. It is important to turn the plant regularly to ensure that all its sides enjoy equal light.

Humidity: This should never be less than 50 per cent and in dry inland areas a humidity tray is a must.

Temperature: Warmth is important for calatheas and the temperature should never drop below 13 °C.

Watering: Water plants frequently in summer, tailing off to keep them barely moist in winter. As tap water tends to mark the leaves of these plants, water under the leaves or spray with rainwater.

Feeding: Regular fortnightly feeds at diluted strength.

Propagation: Calatheas' foliage tends to wither completely in winter, but new growth appears in spring. It is important to divide plants before they start shooting. Each rooted piece of rhizome should be potted into a river sand and imported peat moss mixture, which must never be allowed to dry out until the shoots are looking healthy. Repot into a richer soil.

Uses: Decorative calatheas make fine form plants, either alone or mixed with others in arrangements.

Varieties: *C. makoyana* has strikingly patterned green leaves and green-brown peacock-type markings; *C. zebrina* has velvety green leaves with darker feathery markings; *C. picturata* is a larger variety with light green leaves and darker green markings with purple-brown undersides; *C. picturata* 'Argentea' has pear-shaped, silver leaves with green edges; and *C. ornata* has large green leaves with attractive pink stripes that turn white with age. *C. crocata* is totally different and has more upright leaves and striking orange flowers.

Callisia elegans
Wandering Jew

Habit: Similar in habit to the other wandering Jews (*Tradescantia* varieties and *Zebrina pendula*), callisias, formerly known as *Setcreasea*, have green and white striped leaves with purplish undersides which are slightly larger and more pointed than those of the other members of the family. They need to be pinched back regularly to make a bush. A miniature version, *C. repens,* looks as if it has a golliwog hairstyle when trailing over the sides of a pot.

Soil: Commercial potting soil is ideal, as long as the plants have good drainage.

Light: Callisias need good light or else they become leggy.

Humidity: Callisias enjoy medium humidity but can take dry Highveld climates.

Watering: Keep moist but not soggy and try to water early in the day so that the foliage is not wet overnight.

Feeding: Callisias need no more than a monthly dose of diluted liquid fertiliser.

Propagation: Callisias grow easily from cuttings. Use 12 or more per basket. Dip the ends in hormone powder and grow directly in a potting medium, or root in a mixture of half loam and half river sand and transplant later.

Uses: Callisias are fine hanging trailers that look superb in bright, light, airy areas such as windows or stoeps, either in baskets or containers. They are superb table top plants when well displayed in large ceramic bowls or baskets.

Callisia repens

Chlorophytum comosum

Chlorophytum comosum varieties
Hen and chicks; spider plant

Habit: Indigenous to South Africa, these delightful, easy-to-grow indoor plants produce cheery fountains of grass-like foliage and have proved popular with house plant lovers the world over. Although the mother plant is attractive alone, its main charm is the mass of mini-plants which cascade like spiders on yellow wire-like stems around the central bush. The graceful chlorophytum thrives in a variety of temperatures and grows throughout South Africa. It enjoys being pot-bound.

Soil: Does well in a mixture of equal parts of garden soil, peat moss and river sand, or in any commercial mixture. Mix in half a cup of bone phosphate or a dessertspoonful of general 2:3:2 fertiliser with each bucket of soil.

Light: Needs good light and if grown under artificial light it is important that it should have at least 10 hours of darkness per day for it is a short-day plant.

Humidity: Chlorophytums are not fussy and grow in areas with a high or low humidity.

Watering: Chlorophytums need ample watering in spring and summer with much less in autumn and winter. They must never dry out but will rot if kept soggy or if they have water in the saucer.

Feeding: Give feeds of liquid fertiliser every two months.

Propagation: Separate tubers with a sharp knife or use 'baby spider' offsets. Pin these into a growing mixture while still attached to the mother plant, cutting the stalk between the two only when roots have formed.

Uses: Chlorophytums may be used in baskets or pots anywhere in the house but are particularly effective in bathrooms. Young plants may even be kept underwater in aquariums.

Varieties: *C. comosum* 'Variegatum' has medium green leaves edged with white; *C. comosum* 'Vittatum', the common spider plant, has green leaves with cream central stripes.

Cissus rhombifolia (Rhoicissus rhomboidea)
Grape ivy

Habit: This glossy, good-looking South American vine is the ideal trailer for indoors. Thriving in dim corners, it is the perfect plant for south-facing kitchens and bathrooms which do not get much light. The three-lobed, quilted leaves turn from bronze to deep green and have a soft fuzz on their undersides. This is a no-nonsense plant that should be placed on anybody's list of the ten most successful indoor plants. Like the other members of the *Cissus* genus it has only three dislikes: bright light, peat moss in the soil, and soggy conditions.

Soil: Good loamy, well-drained soil.

Light: Although it will take medium light, it is extremely successful in low light (not dark) positions. Bright light spoils its foliage.

Humidity: Does best with 50 per cent humidity.

Watering: Give deep waterings and allow to drain thoroughly. Leave to become moderately dry before watering again.

Feeding: Liquid fertiliser at diluted strength monthly from spring onwards and every two months from autumn onwards.

Propagation: From single-leaf stem cuttings during any season.

Uses: These vines may be used as trailers or trained up trellises in dim positions where few other plants would succeed.

Varieties: Two other members of the *Cissus* genus well worth growing are *C. antarctica* or kangaroo vine and *C. rhombifolia* 'Ellen Danica'. The former has glossy, serrated leaves on red stalks and grows to a height of 2 m. It is excellent for dim entrance halls but needs a trellis to which its tendrils may cling. *C. rhombifolia* 'Ellen Danica' is similar to *C. rhombifolia* but its sets of leaves are bigger and closer together, making it a much more compact and attractive choice.

Cissus rhombifolia 'Ellen Danica'

Codiaeum variegatum pictum varieties

Codiaeum variegatum pictum
Croton

Habit: One of the most colourful of plants, this bushy and freely branching small shrub thrives in warm, humid places and grows to a metre or more. It offers widely varying leaf shapes and colours. Well-grown crotons are a joy, but they have strict requirements as discussed below.

Below: *Codiaeum* 'Mortimer'
Bottom: *Codiaeum* 'Musaicus'

Soil: Use equal parts of soil, peat moss and river sand enriched with a little well-rotted and sifted kraal manure or SR3:2:1(28) fertiliser.

Light: Very bright light is needed and preferably some sun. Poor light results in loss of colour, which is the plant's best feature. Place it in the sun for a few weeks to regain colour.

Temperature: Although crotons can tolerate some cold, they are happiest in temperatures ranging from 16-28 °C.

Humidity: Above average.

Watering: Keep moist but not soggy. Do not allow crotons to dry out.

Feeding: Feed with liquid food monthly.

Uses: Wonderful colour and specimen plants for containers or indoor gardens. Their height is also an asset.

Varieties: The modern hybrids, all developed from *C. variegatum pictum,* come in many sizes, with differing leaf shapes: broad and oval, long and narrow, lance- or sword-shaped, and straight or curly. Some good modern varieties are: *C.* 'Mrs Iceton', low-growing with small leaves in dominant autumn colours of orange and yellow; *C.* 'Mortimer' with multi-coloured, red-spotted leaves; *C.* 'Musaicus', compact with green and yellow spotted leaves; *C.* 'Excellent' with long, broad green and yellow leaves which slowly change to black and red for dramatic colour effects, 1, 2 m tall; *C.* 'Goldfinger', a compact plant with long, strap-like green and yellow leaves; *C.* 'Arthur Howe' with red, orange and yellow variegated, semi-oak-shaped leaves; *C.* 'Fascination' with yellow variegations on green; and *C.* 'Gold Sun' with small and compact ovate green leaves splattered with yellow markings, 1 m tall, and useful for mixed arrangements.

TIP: Sudden cold weather may cause the leaves of crotons to drop. Should this happen, cut the plant back to two-thirds and move to a warmer spot, then water deeply but less regularly.

Below: *Codiaeum* 'Arthur Howe'
Bottom: *Codiaeum* 'Fascination'

Coffea arabica

Coffea arabica
Coffee plant

Habit: The coffee plant usually grows in the shade of larger trees and is therefore an excellent indoor plant. It has large, shiny, dark green leaves and a handsome, elegant appearance.

Soil: The coffee plant needs light, well-drained soil which contains equal parts of soil, peat moss, sieved compost and clean river sand.

Light: It does well in poorly lit areas, but if you wish to have flowers and even coffee beans, then it requires stronger light, but no sun.

Humidity: Medium to high.

Watering: Water well, then leave until the surface soil dries before watering again.

Feeding: Feed fortnightly with a seaweed liquid food and occasionally spray the leaves with the same fertiliser.

Propagation: Soak fresh seeds in hot water for 24 hours before setting under 2 cm of soil in a pot capable of taking a fairly long taproot.

Uses: The coffee plant is happy in air-conditioned rooms, and therefore a fine choice for offices. Large specimens look very good in floor level pots, while smaller plants look elegant on executive desk tops. It is also ideal for rooms with poor light.

Coleus varieties

Habit: Coleuses are perennials, but are generally grown as annuals. They can hardly be bettered when it comes to the sheer variety and brilliance of colour of their velvety leaves. Hundreds of varieties are available in trays as bedding plants which may be potted out, but their colours are not always the best. It is a good idea to look for varieties grown and sold in pots especially for indoor use.

Soil: Use commercial potting soil or a mixture of equal parts of good garden loam, compost and peat moss.

Light: Best grown in very bright light with only a little early morning or late afternoon sun.

Humidity: Coleuses need medium humidity and should be sprayed regularly or kept on a humidity tray. If the humidity is too low they are inclined to drop their leaves.

Watering: Coleuses enjoy moist conditions, but the soil surface may be allowed to dry slightly between waterings.

Feeding: Coleuses are fairly greedy feeders – provide them with organic or chemical liquid food regularly.

Propagation: Tip cuttings root easily, even in water. Plants also grow easily from seed.

Uses: Mainly used for their brilliant colour.

Varieties: There are a great many of these with a huge variety of colour mixes which are rarely sold by name. In South Africa a lime-green variety known as 'Yellow Perrin' is very popular. The variety *C.* 'Saber' has longer leaves and lasts longer than other varieties as it is slower to form flowers.

Coleus varieties

Cordyline fruticosa varieties

Cordyline fruticosa varieties (*C. terminalis*)

Habit: These colourful modern single-stem varieties with broad leaves are often mistaken for dracaenas. They come in a variety of distinctive blends of pinks and reds, and creams and greens.

Soil: A commercial soil or a good garden loam well mixed with peat moss and compost.

Light: Bright light with a little morning or afternoon sun.

Humidity: Medium. Spray the leaves daily, particularly during hot, dry spells and also sponge them occasionally. Browning of leaf edges generally indicates that the humidity is too low.

Watering: Keep moist but not soggy during their growing period, but rather dry during the cooler months.

Feeding: Use organic liquid fertiliser fortnightly.

Propagation: By stem and tip cuttings.

Uses: Cordylines have a good silhouette and make fine form plants. They are also useful where height is required, and make fine contrast subjects for bold mixed arrangements.

Varieties: The new leaves of *C. fruticosa* 'Red Edge' are more colourful than those lower on the stem and have a very distinct red edging. *C. fruticosa* 'White Edge' is similar to the previous variety except that the edges of the leaves are creamy-white. *C. fruticosa* 'Prince Albert' also has leaves with a red edge but they have solid red patches. *C. fruticosa* 'Kiwi' is a most attractive blend of green, cream and pink. *C. fruticosa* 'Atoom' has large top sprays of pink leaves, while the lower leaves are much darker.

Dieffenbachia amoena 'Tropic Snow'

Dieffenbachia varieties
Dumb-canes

Habit: Indoor dieffenbachias range in height between 1 m and 2 m. They have very erect stems from which broad, fleshy, oval leaves sheath the stalks and spiral upwards. The tips of the leaves generally have a slight downward tilt. They have a built-in shine and are attractively mottled and veined with yellow, cream and white. It is not surprising that these colourful plants have become worldwide favourites.

Soil: Commercial potting soil is ideal, but if you wish to mix your own make it rich, coarse and crumbly, and include old leaves, compost and peat moss.

Humidity: Dieffenbachias prefer normal to high humidity with a higher humidity rate when starting growth in spring. In a too dry atmosphere dieffenbachias are inclined to become infected with red spider and lose their lower leaves. It is a good idea to grow them on a humidity tray and to spray the leaves regularly with water, above and below. Keep dieffenbachias away from fan heaters and radiators in winter.

Light: Filtered light is ideal but they can take fairly dim situations if not overwatered.

Watering: Keep constantly moist but not soggy. Spray the leaves regularly and clean them with a soft sponge. If at all possible, try to use rain water.

Feeding: Feed with organic liquid food every two months.

Propagation: By removing plantlets from the side of the mother plant or by stem cuttings.

Dieffenbachia amoena

Dieffenbachia maculata 'Camilla'

Uses: With their bold leaves and fine form, dieffenbachias are very popular with interior decorators. They are useful as single accent or form plants or in groupings, but be careful to place them in an area where their brittle leaves will not be damaged by passing traffic.

Varieties: New varieties are always coming on the market. The 2 m tall, large-leafed *D. amoena* and *D. amoena* 'Tropic Snow', and the much smaller and more compact but multi-stemmed *D. maculata* 'Camilla' are among the best known. The latter grows to a lush 0,5 m in the home and has taken over the popularity of the old 'Rudolph Roehrs'. Its leaves have a very distinct creamy-white centre with a green-rimmed border. Also multi-stemmed and rather similar, but a better grower and less prone to bacterial diseases, is *D. compacta,* which grows to 0,5 m and has green leaves speckled with cream. A real beauty is 'Hi-color'. It is similar to *D. amoena* 'Tropic Snow' and *D. amoena* but not as stiff. It has less yellow than *D. amoena* 'Tropic Snow' but more than *D. amoena. D. maculata* 'Alexis' is a very low-growing, bushy variety which is rather like a ground cover.

TIP: Because these plants often become leggy, many home gardeners rejuvenate their plants each year or every second season by cutting them back to 10 cm and allowing them to bush. Although it is possible to start a new plant by using the plume of leaves cut from the top, this is really a job for the professionals. With *D. maculata* 'Camilla', *D. maculata* 'Candida' and other multi-stemmed hybrids, it is possible to increase your plants by separation.

Dizygotheca elegantissima (Aralia elegantissima)

Habit: The many-fingered, narrow leaves of these plants change from copper to a purple-black green. They have a much lighter filigree texture than most indoor plants and with their tall stems they live up to their name. Dizygothecas need to be pinched back for a bushy effect.

Soil: Dizygothecas need a loose potting mixture which includes at least 50 per cent organic matter.

Light: Bright light is important or else they become leggy and suffer colour loss. Avoid direct sunlight between 10h00 and 14h00.

Humidity: Medium to high.

Watering: The soil surface should dry out between waterings. If the lower leaves fall off it is a sign of overwatering.

Feeding: Use organic liquid fertiliser monthly.

Propagation: Tip cuttings.

Uses: With their tall and lacy appearance and unusual dark colour, dizygothecas not only provide an excellent contrast when used in plant arrangements, but several grouped together make a striking feature when grown in a container.

Varieties: *D. elegantissima* 'Pollux' is most attractive. It has shorter, broader fronds.

Dizygotheca elegantissima

Dracaena marginata

Dracaena fragrans 'Massangeana'

Dracaena varieties
Corn plants

Habit: This is certainly one of the best low-light plants for interior decoration. These beautiful tropical African plants come in a variety of forms from low, grass-like clumps with attractive striped foliage to the more common tall, dark green giants with strap-like leaves that resemble those of the mealie plant. Leaves vary from narrow to broad. Some are plain green while others have either central stripes or margins of white, cream, yellow and even pink. *D. godseffiana,* the gold-dust dracaena, is a low-growing variety with unusual rounded, speckled leaves.

Soil: Rich loamy soil containing 50 per cent organic matter.

Light: Most dracaenas do best in medium light, but *D. fragrans* and its hybrids thrive in dim light.

Humidity: Average for all dracaenas except *D. marginata* varieties, which prefer a lower humidity.

Watering: Keep moist, rewatering when the surface soil begins to dry. Mist leaves frequently, but in areas with chlorinated water leave the water in an open vessel overnight before use. Do not overwater or the plants will rapidly lose their leaves.

Feeding: Use organic fertiliser every one or two months, either as a foliar feed or in the soil.

Propagation: Tip cuttings and stem segments.

Uses: With their fine form, height and strong lines, these densely foliaged plants are excellent for home and office decoration, especially where light is a problem. *D. godseffiana,* with its spreading nature, looks particularly good in bowl-type containers.

Varieties: There are many of these but among the best known are: *D.* 'Janet Craig nana', a very compact dwarf with

Dracaena deremensis 'White Stripe'

very dark green, glossy leaves; *D. fragrans*, which has broad and handsome dark green leaves, *D. fragrans* 'Massangeana', which is similar to the previous variety but with strong central yellow stripes; *D. fragrans* 'Victoria', with yellow edges and a green central stripe; the various forms of *D. deremensis*, with 'Warneckii' being one of most popular with narrow, light green leaves outlined in white and 'White Stripe' with long green leaves and bold white stripes. *D. marginata* (dragon tree) and *D. marginata* 'Tricolor' are faster growing than most dracaenas and both are extremely elegant with a dense bush of strap-like leaves on top of strong, thin stems giving a striking silhouette. *D. marginata* has maroon-edged leaves while 'Tricolor' is far more exciting with reddish-pink colouring. *D. marginata* 'Colorama' has spiky leaves with tinges of red, pink and yellow. *D. terminalis* 'Firebrand' grows no more than 90 cm tall and has extremely colourful pink and burgundy, spear-shaped, erect leaves with slightly curling tips. *D. deremensis* 'Compacta' has a much fuller appearance than most. As its name suggests, it has leaves grouped far more compactly than some of the other varieties. *D. godseffiana* 'Florida Beauty' has yellow mottled leaves on wiry stems.

TIP: Single plants may look a little spindly, so try grouping several together in a pot or cut out the central stem at a set height to encourage leaf clusters to form around the top, turning it into a ti-plant. It is important to stop the *D. marginata* varieties' growth otherwise they become lank and lose their charm.

Dracaena marginata 'Tricolor'

Dracaena godseffiana 'Florida Beauty'

Dracaena deremensis 'Warneckii'

Fatshedera lizei
Ivy tree

Habit: A hybrid cross between a fatsia and an ivy (*Hedera helix*), this unusual and easy-to-grow indoor plant has the attributes of both of its parents, for it may be grown either as a shrub if it is regularly pinched back or trained to a trellis as a creeper. Should the plant become too large, it is easy to prune back to about 10 cm from the ground. It will then bush out beautifully.

Soil: Either commercial potting soil or equal parts of garden loam, peat moss and river sand plus two teaspoonfuls of SR3:2:1(28) general fertiliser per bucket of mix.

Light: Requires bright light and at least four hours of direct sunlight to thrive, although it will cope with bright light and even artificial light.

Humidity: Average to high humidity. Needs summer temperatures of about 23 °C, but in winter can withstand a drop to about 2 °C.

Watering: Keep barely moist.

Feeding: Use liquid fertiliser quarterly.

Propagation: Use 15 cm long stem cuttings dipped in hormone powder and root in deep containers with a mix of river sand and imported peat moss. Once growing, plant into individual pots and pinch back the tips regularly to encourage bushiness.

Uses: May be grown either as an attractive large-leafed bush for sunny situations or as a creeper.

Varieties: Two attractive variegated kinds are *F. lizei* 'Silver Prince' and *F. lizei* 'Annemieke' which is a blend of lime and dark green.

Fatshedera lizei

Fatsia japonica

Fatsia japonica (Aralia japonica)

Habit: A compact but handsome plant. Its popularity is due to two main features: its glossy, large, dark green palmate leaves, and its undemanding nature. May grow tall, but in the home it rarely tops 1,5 m.

Soil: Use commercial potting soil or a mixture of equal parts of garden loam and organic matter, some river sand and a few teaspoonfuls of superphosphate, ground limestone and SR3:2:1(28) general fertiliser per standard bucket.

Light: This plant enjoys bright light and even a few hours of sun. Put it out under the trees during summer.

Humidity: Medium. Spray when conditions are warm and dry to discourage red spider.

Watering: Keep barely moist except when shooting new growth, at which time they require more liberal amounts of water.

Feeding: Needs little fertilisation, but between October and February you may give some organic liquid food fortnightly.

Propagation: A job best left to the professionals.

Uses: A fine form plant, it is attractive used alone on the floor or in combination with other plants. It may be pruned to any size as it will rapidly produce new growth. Ideal for use in cold homes.

Ficus varieties
Figs

Habit: Three of the over 800 ficus varieties that make exceptional house plants for height and are extremely popular in South Africa are the weeping fig (*F. benjamina*), the rubber plant (*F. elastica* 'Robusta'), and the fiddle-leaf fig (*F. lyrata*). All are fairly fast growing and become quite large plants indoors. They are highly sought after because of their beautiful foliage. Each has very different leaf shapes, but they are generally dark green, although there are also variegated varieties.

Soil: All ficuses need fibrous, well-aerated soil. Half its content should be organic material, with river sand added to the mix and used as a drainage layer at the base of the pot. Do not overpot; they prefer their roots to be snug in the container.

Light: All ficuses do very well in medium light. They are best placed near a window but without direct sunlight.

Humidity: Medium.

Watering: Soak thoroughly, ensuring that the potting mixture is moist all over. Allow to become fairly dry before soaking again. Overwatering is the fig's worst enemy.

Feeding: Fertilise monthly with liquid fertiliser.

Propagation: Air-layering – a professional method – is best for most figs, especially for *F. lyrata*. The others also strike from leaf-bud cuttings taken below a node, with the lower pair of leaves removed.

Uses: Excellent form plants for the home, they are also particularly useful in large offices and the foyers of buildings.

Varieties:

F. benjamina: This variety – today's favourite fig – has much smaller leaves than *F. elastica* and *F. lyrata*. The leaves are generally about 10 cm long and cover the tall arching stems fairly densely, giving the plant an attractive weeping effect. Trained into poodle-tail shapes and made into standards with three or four stems plaited together to create more impressive heads, these are excellent plants for home and office decoration. Planted into attractive tubs, the standards are most striking seen in pairs on either side of a doorway. Leaves tend to drop if the plant is moved to a new location with a different light intensity, but it soon settles down and recovers. *F. benjamina* 'Golden Princess' is a compact variety with cream and green variegated leaves.

F. indica (F. benghaliensis): Similar in style to the *F.*

Ficus elastica 'Robusta'

Ficus benjamina with plaited stems and Christmas decorations

Ficus benjamina in poodle-tail shape with plaited stems

Ficus benjamina 'Golden Princess'

Ficus lyrata

benjamina, but more compact and with even smaller leaves.

***F. elastica* 'Robusta':** For many years the most popular of all large indoor trees, the rubber tree with its strong silhouette makes a superb accent plant. It has glossy, 30 cm long, leathery, dark green oval leaves, and grows to 3 m indoors. This is the most popular form of rubber tree today. The original form *F. elastica* is rarely seen but its replacement *F. elastica* 'Decora' is still grown. Its leaf sheaths and young leaves are maroon, turning to deep green as they age. There is also a variegated form, *F. elastica* 'Europa'. To keep all these varieties bushy, cut them back occasionally.

***F. lyrata*:** Adam is said to have used the leaf of this tree to cover himself when driven from the Garden of Eden. The very large, fiddle-shaped leaves, up to 40 cm long, are glossy with attractive wavy edges. The plants may become quite large but are at their best when young. Older specimens usually keep only the leaves towards the ends of branches, so they should be pruned back to maintain a bushy and attractive appearance. As with all the figs, the leaves must be kept clean, but be gentle with the lyrata's leaves as they are brittle and crack and damage easily.

TIP: Members of the ficus genus all have vigorous root systems and if planted in the ground or brick containers in atriums, may cause damage to bricks, tiles and walls, often lifting and cracking them.

Fittonia varieties
Silver net plant; snakeskin

Habit: Low-creeping fittonias have small, bright green oval leaves with a network of different colour veins, depending on the variety. Colours range from silver and cream to pink and red.

Soil: Normal commercial potting soil or a mix of one part garden soil, one part peat moss and one part river sand.

Light: Will take reasonably dim light. A south-facing window is an ideal position.

Humidity: Above average.

Watering: Keep moist but never soggy.

Feeding: A weak solution of liquid fertiliser fortnightly.

Propagation: Snip off pieces of plant which have rooted while spreading across the surface of the soil. Fittonias root easily.

Uses: Ideal for positions where it can trail slightly, such as bookcases and room dividers or on low coffee tables. Also a good foreground plant in terrariums.

Varieties: *Fittonia verschaffeltii argyroneura* 'Nana' is a smaller but better plant, able to take slightly drier conditions than the larger leafed *F. verschaffeltii argyroneura. F. verschaffeltii* (mosaic plant) also has large leaves with red veins, while *F. verschaffeltii* 'Pearcei' has carmine veins.

Below: *Fittonia verschaffeltii*
Bottom: *Fittonia verschaffeltii argyroneura* 'Nana'

Gibasis geniculata

Gibasis geniculata (*Tradescantia tripogandra* 'Multiflora')
Tahitian bridal veil

Habit: The smallest of the wandering Jew type plants, this mini-leafed variety, from the rain forests of Tahiti, proliferates under good conditions, its string-like stems branching freely. The leaves are dark green with purple undersides. It trails exuberantly over the sides of baskets and produces masses of minute white flowers if grown in an airy position with sufficient light. Pinch back to develop compact, bushy plants.

Soil: Use commercial potting soil.

Light: Medium to bright.

Humidity: Average.

Watering: Allow the surface of the soil to dry between waterings.

Feeding: Overfeeding is worse than underfeeding with these plants. Use diluted liquid food every two months.

Propagation: Use 10 cm long tip cuttings, which root easily. Once transplanted into proper soil, they proliferate and grow fast.

Uses: This miniature is a good choice for baskets in bright, airy positions. It may also be used in terrariums, but unless kept trimmed back, will overpower the rest of the plants.

Hedera helix varieties
Ivy

Habit: In recent years innumerable strains in a great variety of shapes and sizes, ranging from small to very large leafed and in a wide range of colours, have been developed. Consequently this very ancient plant is as popular today as it was in Homeric times. Ivies can be ruffled, curled, wavy, cupped, plain, simple, and large or miniature, with different combinations of green tinged with white, yellow, cream and even pink. Although it has changed considerably over the years, the ivy remains untemperamental and easy to grow. The small-leafed varieties are best suited to use indoors. Prune to 15 cm when young to encourage bushy growth.

Soil: Ordinary potting soil is ideal, but it may be improved by adding some leaf mould and well-rotted kraal manure.

Light: Ivy enjoys about four hours of sunlight a day, but for the rest it prefers cool shade. Green varieties are able to take more sun than some of the variegated forms.

Watering: Water well during spring and summer but reduce the quantity in winter.

Feeding: Monthly, from spring to the end of summer, using a good liquid fertiliser.

Propagation: Easy to root in water. Cuttings take well at most times of the year, but particularly in spring.

Uses: Having adhesive roots, ivy is ideal for growing up walls, and can be easily trained up trellises. It looks spectacular when grown in baskets. Ideal in plant arrangements. Needs a bright, airy position indoors.

Varieties: There are a huge number, but among the best and most popular are: *Hedera helix,* the common green ivy known as English ivy; *H. helix* 'Glacier', a variegated English ivy; *H. helix* 'Pittsburgh', which is similar to *H. helix* 'Glacier', but with plain dark green leaves; *H. canariensis* 'Gloire de Merengo', which has large variegated green and white leaves; *H. helix* 'Golden Heart', which has green leaves with a bright yellow centre; *H. helix* 'Curlilocks', which has medium green leaves with curled edges; *H. helix* 'Marmorata', which has light green leaves, speckled with cream; and *H. helix* 'Harold' which has variegated green and white leaves.

Below, left: *Hedera canariensis* 'Gloire de Merengo'
Bottom, left: *Hedera helix* 'Pittsburgh'
Below, right: *Hedera helix* 'Glacier'
Bottom, right: *Hedera helix* 'Marmorata'

Hypoestes varieties

Hypoestes sanguinolenta
Polka-dot plant

Habit: Known as freckle face in Britain, this charming plant is a fast grower. It has light green leaves dusted with pink spots. Keep pruned back at all times to retain a compact growth habit, otherwise it becomes lank. It is particularly attractive when young and is best treated as an annual.

Soil: Commercial potting soil is ideal, or use a good loam-based soil which includes some compost.

Light: This should be as bright as possible, even with some direct sunlight to ensure that the plant keeps its pink colouring, otherwise the leaves become green.

Humidity: It does best with average (25 per cent) to medium humidity. Use a humidity tray.

Watering: Important to keep moist, but not soggy, with slightly less water in winter.

Feeding: Feed monthly with liquid fertiliser.

Propagation: By seed in spring or stem cuttings in summer.

Uses: Ideal where a low ground cover type plant is needed. Looks beautiful in flat bowls or in the foreground in plant arrangements.

Varieties: *H. sanguinolenta* 'Pink Splash' is a very attractive variety showing a lot more pink. Two distinctive new varieties are *H.* 'Red Spot', which has a much richer colouring, and *H.* 'White Spot' which has striking green and white leaves.

Leea guineens

Leea guineens

Habit: New to this country, the leea has become very popular overseas in recent years. Upright and elegant, it has a very good shape and is densely covered with small, attractive leaves. Although small red flowers are formed, the plant's biggest asset is its beautifully shaped, coloured leaves.

Soil: Enjoys a fairly firm soil mixture which should include a fair amount of peat moss.

Light: Requires the best possible light without actual direct sunlight.

Humidity: Average.

Watering: Keep fairly moist, allowing just the surface soil to dry slightly before watering again.

Feeding: Feed with liquid food weekly.

Uses: A fine contrast plant for groupings. It also looks very good alone.

Propagation: By seed.

Varieties: The two most popular varieties are *L. guineens* 'Rubra', which is green and compact with a green stem, and *L. guineens* 'Burgundy', which is taller, has a red stem and new, solid burgundy leaves, changing slowly to green-tinged red.

Maranta leuconeura
Prayer plant

Habit: Spectacular, colourful foliage is the main feature of this group of plants. Their oval leaves have prominent, coloured veins or prominent splotches of colour. Related to calatheas, the marantas are, however, lower growing. Their common name is derived from their strange habit of closing and raising their leaves at night, almost in an attitude of prayer. Warmth is important to these plants and they hate draughts and direct sunlight. They benefit from a change of scene and it's a good idea occasionally to put them outside in a shady area during the warm months.

Soil: Equal parts of garden loam, peat moss and river sand, together with two teaspoonfuls of superphosphates and two teaspoonfuls of general fertiliser to a standard bucketful of soil.

Light: Bright filtered light.

Humidity: High.

Watering: The root ball must never dry out. Water liberally during the growing season, and sparingly from March to August.

Feeding: Diluted liquid fertiliser fortnightly during summer.

Propagation: Best by cuttings.

Uses: Colourful additions to the indoor scene, either alone on coffee tables or included in plant arrangements.

Varieties: *M. bicolor* grows 30 cm tall and has dark leaves marked with pale brown blotches. *M. leuconeura kerchoviana* is similar to *M. bicolor* but even more colourful. It has emerald green leaves with striking red-brown splotches, plus interestingly marked undersides to the leaves. *M. leuconeura erythroneura* (often called *M. leuconeura tricolor* in South Africa) has dark green leaves 'painted' with intricate red-brown, feather-like markings.

Maranta leuconeura erythroneura

Monstera deliciosa

Monstera deliciosa
Delicious monster

Habit: Sturdy support is important for this large-leafed climber. A great favourite for indoors, its heart-shaped leaves, often 30 cm wide, are both perforated and deeply cut. Aerial roots are a feature of this plant and although a certain number may be removed, the rest should be covered with compost or pushed into a thick moss stick and kept moist.

Soil: Equal parts of garden loam, or commercial potting soil and peat moss, with some river sand.

Light: Bright filtered light, but may take some sun.

Humidity: Average.

Watering: Water well and then allow the surface soil to dry slightly before watering again. Never allow the root ball to dry out.

Feeding: Feed with liquid fertiliser only two or three times during the growing season – not in winter.

Propagation: From a leaf bud with one mature leaf, from stem cuttings, by seed and by air layering.

Uses: An easy-to-grow house plant, it is ideal for placing in an area where a substantial plant is needed – its stem may reach 6 m even indoors.

Peperomia caperata

Peperomia varieties

Habit: Grown mainly for their attractive leaves, which are often quilted, this is a large and varied genus. Not all are suitable as house plants, but a great many are – from small-leafed, slightly trailing varieties to those with large and glossy upright leaves. Nearly all are neat and compact.

Soil: Peperomias prefer a peat mixture, almost without soil, with only one part commercial potting soil to equal parts compost and imported peat moss. The mixture should be light and well aerated.

Light: Medium light.

Humidity: Medium to high during hot weather, but may be less during cooler months.

Watering: Water well, then allow to become moderately dry before watering again. Underwater them rather than allow them to be soggy. Ensure good drainage.

Feeding: Feed fortnightly with diluted liquid fertiliser.

Propagation: There are two methods: use tip cuttings for those with stems, otherwise leaf cuttings.

Uses: Ideal small foliage plants for desk tops, shelves and coffee tables. Excellent for bottle gardens.

Varieties: Good varieties are: *P. hederifolia* (*P. marmorata*) with silver-green leaves; *P. caperata* with small dark green, rippled leaves and *P. caperata* 'Emerald Ripple' with dark green, heart-shaped, well-veined and rippled leaves; *P.* 'Red Ripple' with orange leaves; *P. obtusifolia* 'USA' with waxy light green leaves with broad cream borders; *P.* 'Julii' which is similar to 'USA' but with pinkish-red leaf borders and undersides; *P. obtusifolia* 'Greengold', a compact, dark green variety marbled with creamy-yellow; *P. sandersii*, the watermelon peperomia, glossy-leafed, with colours changing from pale green to blue-green; *P. scandens*, a delightful trailing variety also available in a variegated form; *P. metallica* which has quilted, heart-shaped leaves with a metallic lustre; and *P. griseo-argentea*, the ivy peperomia, which has small, round, deeply grooved and rippled purple-olive coloured leaves.

TIP: Small peperomias are ideal for using in arrangements and particularly in terrariums, but with no drainage in these bowls it is vital not to overwater, otherwise they will drop their leaves.

Peperomia sandersii

Peperomia hederifolia

Peperomia caperata 'Emerald Ripple'

Peperomia scandens

Peperomia 'Red Ripple'

Peperomia 'Julii'

Peperomia 'USA'

Philodendron scandens

Philodendron scandens
Sweetheart creeper

Habit: This is one of the easiest climbers for the home. It can grow magnificently, if given just a little tender loving care. First of all, it should be kept bushy by continually nipping out growing tips, and secondly, the leaves need to be wiped clean occasionally with a damp cloth. This climber, with its large heart-shaped leaves, is ideal for growing in large entrance halls or stairwells. Prune when necessary.

Soil: Mix equal parts of garden loam, compost and river sand plus a tablespoon each of superphosphate, limestone and a general fertiliser like SR3:2:1(28), or use any general-purpose commercial potting soil, adding a little fertiliser as with the home blend.

Light: Provide filtered light without direct sunlight.

Humidity: Medium.

Watering: Water deeply, then allow the soil to dry to the touch before watering again.

Feeding: Feed every two months with liquid fertiliser from spring to autumn, either through the soil or with foliar feeding.

Propagation: By division, or from cuttings of stems or growing tips.

Uses: Excellent for medium light conditions, it may be trained to grow up trellises or trail from baskets.

Philodendron selloum

Habit: Growing into a very large, bold plant with impressive, deeply cut, glossy leaves radiating from a central short, stout stem, the selloum needs a lot of space indoors. For impact it is best seen alone rather than with other plants. A feature of this plant is its large aerial roots which can be ugly or inconvenient, so try to direct them into the soil. Only in extreme cases should any of these roots be removed.

Soil: Equal parts of fibrous soil, humus and river sand.

Light: Philodendrons enjoy medium bright light and may even have some sun.

Humidity: Average.

Watering: May be kept reasonably dry. Allow to dry out before watering again. The dimmer the light, the less water needed.

Feeding: Use slow-release fertiliser such as SR3:2:1(28) quarterly.

Propagation: Usually by seed or air layering.

Uses: These rather majestic plants are best used as architectural form plants in large buildings, as they can be overpowering in smaller rooms.

Philodendron selloum

Philodendron varieties

Habit: This wide-ranging genus offers a variety of fast-growing forms, some creeping, some upright and some with great, deeply lobed leaves. Many have large, arrow-shaped leaves, while others are small and heart-shaped. All are glossy and attractive, and most make excellent indoor plants.

Soil: General-purpose commercial potting soil is ideal, or mix equal parts of garden loam, leaf mould and river sand in a bucket. To this add a tablespoon each of superphosphate, limestone and SR3:2:1(28) fertiliser.

Light: Medium to bright light without sunlight.

Humidity: High.

Watering: Water well and then allow the soil to dry to the touch before watering again.

Feeding: Use liquid fertiliser every two months during spring and summer.

Propagation: Stem cuttings, growing tips or by division.

Uses: Some are ideal as large creepers with dramatically attractive leaves. Whether creeping or upright, they all make excellent accent plants where space is available.

Varieties: These include: *P. erubescens* 'Red Emerald', with great arrow-shaped, maroon-backed leaves; *P.* 'Red Duchess', a dark green, glossy-leafed variety with red undersides, which was developed for office use; *P. laciniatum,* a hardy variety with triangular-shaped leaves; *P. futura* which looks very much like a miniature delicious monster; and *P.* 'Florida', which has a slender, climbing stem with soft, leathery, deep green leaves, brown-red on the reverse. Another beauty is the fiddle leaf philodendron *(P. panduraeforme),* which has attractive fiddle-shaped, leathery, olive green leaves. Two other varieties with striking leaf forms are *P.* 'Burgundy', with lovely red new growth which turns to large dark green leaves and *P. hastatum* 'Red Emerald', with arrow-shaped, medium green leaves.

Philodendron futura

Philodendron laciniatum

Philodendron erubescens 'Red Emerald'

Pilea cadierei
Aluminium plant

Habit: A compact plant with varieties ranging between 10 and 30 cm in height. It gained its common name due to the fact that its interesting, plump leaves, which have a quilted appearance with sunken veins, appear to have been brushed with aluminium paint.

Soil: Commercial potting soil or any light, porous soil which includes some peat moss and other organic material is ideal.

Light: Indirect or filtered light. Legginess is a sign of too little light.

Humidity: Pileas enjoy some humidity during growing stages but later prefer rather drier conditions.

Watering: Keep barely moist in summer and a little drier in winter.

Feeding: Regular feeding with half-strength liquid fertiliser is desirable during the growing season.

Propagation: Pileas are so easy to grow from cuttings or self-sown plantlets that they should be treated as annuals.

Uses: Ideal terrarium plants and plants for arrangements. Also ideal for living room decoration on coffee tables and windowsills, or on office desks or counters.

Varieties: A number of pilea forms have resulted in some interesting common names such as artillery plant and friendship plant, but the modern varieties today include *P. spruceana* (silver tree) which has green serrated leaves with a central aluminium-coloured stripe; *P. spruceana* 'Norfolk', which has pinkish blobs on the aluminium when the plant is growing well; and *P. involucrata* 'Moon Valley', with bright green, puckered leaves with dark veins.

Below: *Pilea spruceana* 'Norfolk'
Bottom: *Pilea cadierei*

Pisonia brunonia 'Variegata'

Pisonia brunonia 'Variegata'

Habit: Not unlike a variegated rubber plant in appearance, these upright tropical plants have bold and attractive, marbled creamy-white variegations on large leaves that are up to 30 cm long. They grow easily indoors, usually reaching a height of about 3,5 m.

Soil: Commercial potting soil or a mixture of equal parts of garden loam and peat moss or leaf mould.

Light: Flourishes in good light with some sun.

Humidity: Medium to high. Above normal during the growing season.

Watering: Moderate during the growing season, decreasing in winter. Never allow to dry out.

Feeding: Feed occasionally with liquid fertiliser during summer.

Propagation: Grows easily from cuttings.

Uses: Ideal where tall plants are needed in bright positions.

Plectranthus australis

Plectranthus australis
Money plant

Habit: Popular as a ground cover, this fast-growing plant makes an excellent indoor plant, either in a pot or hanging basket. *Plectranthus australis* develops long, trailing stems in a matter of months. Its leaves are an attractive green and it produces delicate white flowers, but it is grown for its foliage, not its flowers.

Soil: The plectranthus is not very particular and will do well in a commercial potting soil or in your own blend of one part garden loam, one part peat moss or leaf mould and one part river sand.

Light: A plectranthus can take sunlight but does best in bright, filtered light.

Humidity: Low.

Watering: Enjoys moist conditions and should not be allowed to dry out.

Feeding: Use liquid fertiliser regularly either in the soil or as foliar feed during the spring/summer growing season.

Propagation: Easy to grow from cuttings, which root quickly in water.

Uses: Fine trailing specimen for 25-30 cm aero-bowls or pinched back to make a full plant for a bowl on a low table.

Pleomele reflexa variegata

Pleomele reflexa variegata
Song of India

Habit: This slow-growing plant with arching stems has narrow, short leaves which look like those of *Dracaena deremensis*. The leaves have green centres and creamy-yellow margins and they spiral around the stem. It takes them many years to reach their full height of about 1,5 m.

Soil: Drainage is most important with this plant and the soil should contain at least 50 per cent organic matter and some river sand, with a little well-rotted manure.

Light: This variegated form enjoys fairly good light.

Humidity: About 25 per cent.

Watering: Water well, then leave to become fairly dry before drenching again. Never allow to stand in water.

Feeding: Liquid food regularly during the growing season, but none during the cold months.

Propagation: Plantlets grow easily from 10 cm long tip or stem cuttings planted in a mixture of half river sand and half peat moss.

Uses: Ideal for coffee tables and other table tops when small, these slow growers eventually develop striking sculptural forms and make excellent accent plants.

Varieties: Less exciting and not seen as often, but nonetheless a most attractive plant, especially for poor light positions, is the green version *P. reflexa,* known in America as *Dracaena reflexa.*

Polyscias fruticosa 'Ming'
Aralia 'Ming'

Habit: A miniature multi-stemmed aralia with fine, small leaves, the 'Ming' is well named, for it looks very much like the plants seen in ancient Chinese paintings.

Soil: Provide aralias with a light, well-drained soil which includes 50 per cent organic matter such as chopped bark, compost and peat moss, together with good, friable garden loam.

Light: Excellent for medium light positions.

Humidity: Medium to high.

Watering: Allow the soil surface to dry out between waterings. Ensure that no water collects in the saucer beneath the plant.

Feeding: Needs regular monthly liquid and foliar feeding during its growing months.

Propagation: Tip cuttings.

Uses: Quaint and striking, this beautiful little plant is a fine form plant for indoor decoration. It looks good in a bowl and particularly in a ceramic one with a Chinese motif, which will give it a rather bonsai-like appearance.

Polyscias fruticosa 'Ming'

Saxifraga stolonifera

Saxifraga stolonifera
Mother-of-thousands

Habit: Like a hen and chicks, this small plant develops masses of small plantlets trailing from the mother plant on slender threads over 50 cm long. It has attractive geranium-like, blue-green leaves with a touch of silver.

Soil: Needs a light, well-drained and aerated soil which contains half compost or peat moss and some river sand.

Light: Does best in a medium light position.

Humidity: Average.

Watering: Keep moist but allow the surface to dry slightly before watering again. If hanging in a breezy position, check regularly to ensure that it does not dry out.

Feeding: Feed monthly with liquid fertiliser during the growing season.

Propagation: Multiplies easily when small plants hanging from the side of the plant are pinned into the growing medium. The little plants root rapidly. The mother plant may also be divided.

Uses: Makes an attractive plant for a hanging basket. It also makes a fine ground cover for other pot plants. Children are usually fascinated by the 'babies', and enjoy planting them.

Varieties: *S. stolonifera* 'Tricolor' has touches of green, white and pink on its leaves.

Schefflera actinophylla

Schefflera actinophylla (Brassia actinophylla)

Umbrella tree

Habit: This is one of the finest and easiest trees to grow in not too dim indoor positions. Large, glossy green leaves, rather like hands with extended fingers, radiate in mounds from a single stem, forming a striking, billowy green canopy. May reach a height of 3 m and deserves an uncramped position.

Soil: For best results use a light soil which includes at least half organic matter. If using potting soil add extra compost.

Light: Although it will grow in full sunlight, it does very well in medium light positions indoors.

Humidity: Medium.

Watering: Do not overwater – soak thoroughly and then leave until almost dry before watering again.

Feeding: Feed fortnightly with liquid fertiliser during spring and summer.

Propagation: This is hardly a job for the amateur gardener. Generally done by seed, but tricky to germinate.

Uses: One of the tallest and fullest of indoor trees, they make excellent specimen plants and are well displayed behind settees and in other positions where bold height is needed.

Schefflera arboricola 'Gold Capella'

Schefflera arboricola (Brassia arboricola)

Miniature umbrella plant

Habit: Among the most popular of indoor plants, this small tree has attractive, glossy leaves similar to those of its big brother *S. actinophylla*, but grows to only about a third of its size. Though attractive on its own if pinched back regularly, it is more decorative when grouped in threes to create a very full effect. Should plants become leggy, do not hesitate to cut them back – they respond very well, growing quickly and becoming much more bushy. New variegated varieties of this plant are in great demand.

Soil: Commercial potting soil boosted with additional organic material such as leafmould or compost in a ratio of two to one is ideal.

Light: Thrives in medium to bright light positions.

Humidity: Medium.

Watering: Soak thoroughly, then leave till almost dry before watering again.

Feeding: Use liquid fertilisers fortnightly throughout the active growing season, i.e. from spring through to the end of autumn.

Schefflera arboricola

Propagation: Best done professionally with seed – not a job for amateurs.

Uses: An ideal medium-height specimen plant that mixes well with other plants in arrangements and groupings. Variegated forms make excellent contrast plants.

Varieties: Green-leaf types include *S. arboricola* 'Compacta', a hardy, good grower, and *S. arboricola* 'Clementine', another hardy variety with a crinkly leaf. Variegated forms include *S. arboricola* 'Capella' with yellow markings towards the tips; *S.arboricola* 'Green Gold' with yellow variegations throughout its leaves; *S. arboricola* 'Gold Capella' with most leaves variegated yellow and green, but many solid yellow; *S. arboricola* 'Jacqueline' with crinkly leaves with yellow outer edges; and *S. arboricola* 'Trinette' with distinctive yellow markings.

Scindapsus aureus (Epipremnum aureum)

Devil's ivy

Habit: Rather like the *Philodendron scandens*, but with attractive, broad, glossy, and ornamental green and yellow leaves, the devil's ivy is an ideal indoor trailer or climber. It is one of the few variegated-leafed plants that keeps its colour even in fairly dim light conditions.

Soil: Enjoys a peat-based soil. Mix three parts peat moss to one part garden soil, or add two parts peat moss to a commercial potting soil.

Light: Although it enjoys bright filtered light it does surprisingly well in poor light.

Humidity: Thrives in humid conditions. In dry areas it should either be misted regularly or grown on a humidity tray which is half-filled with water. Ensure, however, that the plant does not actually stand in water.

Watering: Water thoroughly but then allow the plant to become moderately dry before watering again.

Feeding: These plants are not heavy feeders – it is only necessary to use liquid fertiliser quarterly.

Propagation: Use stem cuttings with one leaf. May be propagated at any time, but most successful in spring and summer.

Uses: Useful either as a pot or basket plant, it may be trained on a trellis or allowed to trail from a basket.

Varieties: Other popular varieties are *S. aureus* 'Marble Queen', which has almost totally white leaves, with only a little green, and *S. aureus* 'Golden Queen', which has bold swirls of yellow.

TIP: To encourage large leaves, it is important to keep the air roots moist. This is best done by training them into a pole made of wire mesh and filled with sphagnum moss or coir. If kept moist, the plants will grow faster.

Scindapsus aureus

Selaginella varieties

Selaginella varieties

Sweat plants

Habit: This is a large genus of creeping plants with feathery leaves, available in a great variety of greens. They root on the surface and branch rapidly in steamy conditions – hence their common name. Their nature makes them excellent candidates for terrariums.

Soil: Provide with a loose, friable soil mixture containing equal parts of soil, compost and river sand.

Light: These plants enjoy bright light and do best near a window, but without direct sun.

Humidity: High.

Watering: Keep moist at all times. Though they must never dry out, they do not enjoy soggy conditions.

Feeding: Feed very occasionally with diluted liquid fertiliser.

Propagation: Best grown from self-rooted fronds in shallow trays containing a mixture of peat moss and river sand. Create a humid atmosphere by covering the container with clear plastic.

Uses: May be grown alone in pots, but are a perfect foreground ground cover for terrarium arrangements.

Varieties: These include: *S. apoda*, low-growing with dull green foliage; *S. caulescens*, taller with lime green leaves; *S. emmeliana*, light green; emerald green *S. kraussiana* (club moss); *S. martensii*, bright green with white varigations on the leaf edges; and *S. uncinata*, with blue-green foliage.

Soleirolia soleirolii

Soleirolia soleirolii (Helxine soleirolii)

Peace-in-the-home; baby's tears

Habit: With leaves no bigger than a baby's tears, this plant probably has the smallest leaves in the indoor plant world. This little charmer is a most rewarding ground cover for the home. Mounding in the centre, its minute light green leaves hang in strings over the edge of the pot.

Soil: Enjoys a soil rich in humus. Mix equal parts of good garden loam and peat moss.

Light: As bright as possible without sun.

Humidity: Average.

Watering: The soil must be moist at all times, but never soggy. Water early in the day to ensure that the foliage is never wet at night.

Feeding: Use diluted liquid food monthly.

Propagation: Division of plants is the easiest way, but 8 cm long tip cuttings also grow well if first rooted in trays of half sand and half peat moss.

Uses: Makes a good ground cover grown around larger indoor plants, softening the edges of containers. It also does well in terrariums but needs to be watched or it will exuberantly take over.

Varieties: There are two other beautiful varieties, worth looking out for: the pale lime green *S. soleirolii* 'Aurea', and *S. soleirolii* 'Variegata' which is green and white.

Spathiphyllum wallisii

Spathiphyllum wallisii

Peace lily; white flag

Habit: A member of the arum family, the spathiphyllum has typical white spathe flowers. Flowering for nearly a month in spring and often again in autumn, it produces a fountain of dense, shiny, dark green lance-shaped leaves.

Soil: Half imported peat moss and half good garden loam produces the best mixture for this hungry plant.

Light: Useful for shady and even quite dark situations.

Humidity: Does best with high humidity and needs frequent misting in hot and dry inland areas.

Watering: Requires moist conditions at all times – but don't allow it to became soggy or stand in a saucer filled with water.

Feeding: A greedy feeder, it is almost impossible to overfeed. Provide weekly with either liquid organic food or spray the leaves with foliar feed.

Propagation: By division when repotting or by seed.

Uses: As one of the few plants that flowers even in fairly dim conditions, it is an ideal house plant that glows with health at all times. Ideal for displaying on coffee tables or shelves, it also mixes well in plant arrangements.

Varieties: *S.* 'Clevelandii' is slightly larger and less compact than *S. wallisii. S.* 'Mauna Loa', with larger flowers, grows to about 60 cm tall, making it an ideal floor plant. It has all the qualities of *S. wallisii* except that it is taller and the leaves are not as dense. Among the newer varieties a particularly good, more compact type is *S.* 'Queen Amazonica'.

Stereospernum danielle

Stromanthe amabilis

Stereospernum danielle (Radermachera danielle)

Habit: Too new to have a common name, this East Asian plant is fast increasing in popularity. A tall and elegantly erect plant with small, attractive, glossy green leaves, it is a hardy, unfussy and strong grower. Though it has no flowers, it is nonetheless decorative, with a compact growth habit which makes it a splendid indoor plant.

Soil: Enjoys a well-drained soil such as commercial potting soil, but should have a little lime added.

Light: Medium to full light and even some early morning or late afternoon sun.

Humidity: Unfussy.

Watering: Must never dry out. It enjoys a fair amount of moisture without being soggy, especially in very light areas.

Feeding: Feed weekly with a good liquid food.

Propagation: By seeds or cuttings, but the latter is not recommended.

Uses: Looks great as a single specimen accent plant or grouped with others in an arrangement.

Stromanthe amabilis

Habit: Similar in practically every way to the marantas and calatheas, this attractive plant with its charming arrangement of light and dark greens in its leaves that look like peacock feathers is an excellent choice for the home. Easier to grow than its near relatives, it forms compact mounds, and has a more open-leafed appearance.

Soil: Enjoys a slightly acid soil – include some extra peat moss with normal commercial potting soil.

Light: A shade lover, it may take a little early morning or late afternoon sun during the cooler months, but is best grown in bright light without direct sun for the rest of the year.

Humidity: Normal.

Watering: The plant must never totally dry out, but allow the surface to dry slightly between waterings.

Feeding: Feed fortnightly with liquid fertiliser during the warmer growing months.

Propagation: Separate the creeping rhizomes in spring and plant out in trays until rooted, then plant into small pots.

Uses: Attractive alone or in small arrangements, they also make good subjects for terrariums.

Syngonium podophyllum 'White Butterfly'

Goose foot plant

Habit: This is one of the finest plants for indoors. It has shiny, creamy-white leaves edged with green and needs similar treatment to philodendrons. They change in appearance as they age, their arrow-shaped leaves becoming smaller over the years. Leaves at different stages of growth are often found on one plant. They develop into even more attractive plants if trimmed regularly.

Soil: May be grown in any general-purpose potting soil.

Light: Needs bright, filtered light or at least 10 hours of artificial light. In dim light it will continue to grow, but will lose its colouring.

Humidity: Medium.

Watering: Keep moist.

Feeding: Being heavy feeders, they should be given liquid food weekly during the warm months and fortnightly during winter.

Propagation: Grow easily from stem cuttings, taken just below a node and grown in a mixture of half peat moss and half river sand. Repot in August or September only when necessary.

Uses: Syngoniums are ideal for growing from a hanging basket, and also grow well against moss poles, but need to be trained and have their roots hidden in the coir.

Varieties: There are a number of other attractive variegated varieties, but the best of the solid greens is *S. podophyllum* 'Emerald Green' which has lovely shiny leaves with a slight yellowish tinge.

Syngonium podophyllum 'White Butterfly'

Tradescantia albiflora 'Tricolor'

Tradescantia albiflora 'Laekenensis'

Tradescantia albiflora

***Tradescantia* varieties**
Wandering Jew

Habit: Attractive, easy-to-grow trailing plants with striking variegated leaves. Prune to keep neat and bushy. With coloured varieties always remove plain green leaves or the entire plant may revert to green.

Soil: Any good commercial potting soil will do, provided there is good drainage.

Light: As bright as possible for the best results.

Humidity: Normal, about 25 per cent.

Watering: Tradescantias hate soggy conditions. Allow the surface soil to dry out between waterings.

Feeding: Feed with liquid fertiliser every two months.

Propagation: Cuttings strike in virtually any soil and grow almost immediately.

Uses: Ideal subjects for filling wall niches, hanging baskets and all sorts of pots and containers where you need a trailing effect.

Varieties: There are a great many of these, but some of the best are: *T. fluminensis*, considered the true wandering Jew, with shiny, mid-green leaves streaked with creamy white; *T. albiflora* 'Tricolor,' which has lovely lilac shading and *T. albiflora* 'Laekenensis', with cream and lilac leaves; *T. fluminensis* 'Quicksilver', which is a greatly improved form with bold cream and green markings and a rather silvery sheen; and *T. blossfeldiana*, which has attractive purple, cream and green markings.

Yucca elephantipes
Dagger plant

Habit: This is an ideal form plant. Yuccas, usually grown as ti-plants, are extremely striking novelties created by pruning back the stout single stems of the plants at a set height to stunt their growth, yet at the same time encouraging the crowns of the leaves to cluster around the point of the cutting. Yuccas may be presented as single-stemmed plants or as groups of three in a single pot, each pruned to a different height. *Y. elephantipes* has spineless, blue-green leaves.

Soil: Commercial potting soil is ideal, otherwise mix one part garden soil, one part humus or peat moss and one part river sand. Also place a layer of river sand at the bottom of the pot to ensure good drainage.

Light: Bright light is important for growth and yuccas need some sunlight daily to develop properly.

Humidity: Low.

Watering: Water thoroughly and then leave until almost dry before watering again. They can tolerate some drying out.

Feeding: Avoid overfeeding. Generally quarterly, but you may give a little more organic liquid food during the spring/summer growing period.

Propagation: May be done by seed, by offsets attached to the plants, by 30 cm long tip cuttings or by stem sections of 45 cm or more.

Uses: Strikingly decorative, providing excellent silhouettes where form and accent are needed.

Yucca elephantipes

Zebrina pendula 'Quadricolor'

Zebrina pendula 'Quadricolor'
Wandering Jew

Habit: A superbly coloured plant, which in South Africa is the most commonly known wandering Jew, although several others, such as *Tradescantia* varieties and *Callisia elegans* are also known by this common name. It has a mixture of green and purple leaves with silvery striped markings on the upper leaves and a vivid purple underneath.

Soil: Commercial potting soil.

Light: Best possible.

Humidity: Average, about 25 per cent.

Watering: Allow the surface to become dry to the touch before rewatering. Always ensure good drainage, as wandering Jews dislike being too wet.

Feeding: Liquid fertiliser every two months.

Propagation: Grows very easily from cuttings.

Uses: Extremely decorative, and useful wherever a colourful trailing effect is necessary. Very attractive in bright bathrooms.

5. Ferns

Adiantum varieties
Maidenhair fern

Habit: With a soft, billowy appearance, the lacy fronds of the maidenhair fern are made up of many delicate, bright green, fan-shaped leaves, showing up well on shiny black, wiry stems. Though relatively easy to grow, many people seem to struggle with them. This is generally because they are kept in stuffy, airless conditions. Being tropical plants, they need high humidity, but do best in cool, airy but not draughty rooms. There are many different maidenhair fern varieties, some of which are very fine, some with a pink tinge, and others with slightly ruffled leaves.

Soil: Maidenhair ferns enjoy humus-enriched soil with some lime. The texture should be loose, well drained and fibrous, and should include river sand, peat moss and bark.

Light: Bright but no direct sun. Can also take reasonably dim light.

Humidity: Maidenhair ferns enjoy high humidity and are best grown on a humidity tray. Lack of humidity causes wilting or browning of the fronds.

Watering: Keep moist but not soggy.

Feeding: Use special slow-release fern foods now available as spikes or in powder form, or use weak solutions of liquid fertiliser directly into the soil – never over the leaves.

Propagation: By division or spores.

Uses: Either as striking accent plants in a pot or basket or for softening the edges of plant groupings. They look lovely on low tables.

Varieties: *A. aethiopicum* is known as the common maidenhair fern but is rarely sold commercially now because of the improved varieties such as *A. raddianum* 'Brilliant Else', which is a dense, bushy and bigger variety. A smaller bushy version is *A. raddianum* 'Fritzluthii', while *A. raddianum* 'Monocolor' is less bushy, but with longer leaves. *A. hispidulum* has rose-tipped leaves.

Adiantum raddianum

Asplenium bulbiferum
Mother's fern

Habit: Unlike *A. nidus*, this Mauritian variety is tufted, with fine lacy leaves. Small bulblets grow on these leaves, which form new plants when rooted.

Soil: Add peat moss to any commercial potting soil mix.

Light: Needs good light but certainly no sun between 10h00 and 17h00.

Humidity: Enjoys high humidity, growing best on a humidity tray in dry areas.

Watering: Keep moist, except in winter when less water is needed.

Feeding: Use special slow-release fern fertilisers or organic liquid food every two months.

Propagation: Plant bulbils attached to leaves.

Uses: An ideal plant for terrariums, pots and indoor gardens.

Asplenium bulbiferum

Asplenium nidus

Asplenium nidus
Birdsnest fern

Habit: The fresh green, satiny-smooth and spatula-shaped large leaves are without any 'feathers' and are totally unlike those of normal ferns. They form a circle around a black nest-like centre of black hair, which gives this fern its common name. Under ideal conditions its fronds may top a metre in length. Its undivided fronds are extremely sensitive to the touch – particularly when small – so do not handle them and avoid contact with neighbouring plants which may scar the leaves. They dislike leaf cleaning sprays and polishes; rather syringe occasionally with water.

Soil: A loose, well-drained peat mixture.

Light: A shady, reasonably dim position to keep the leaves at their best. Ideal in a south window.

Humidity: An ideal house plant, the birdsnest fern can take slightly drier air conditions than many other ferns.

Watering: Keep moist, but during winter allow the surface to dry out between waterings.

Feeding: Do not overfeed. Use a weak solution of organic liquid food quarterly.

Propagation: From spores at any time.

Uses: Birdsnest ferns do well in pots and are very successful in indoor gardens where they may grow unhampered to their full height.

Cyrtomium falcatum
Holly fern

Habit: Bold, with large, dark green, holly-like leaflets on dense, strong, arching stems up to 60 cm long. This is one of the best ferns for indoors, with many attributes including its good looks in its favour. It succeeds in conditions other ferns could not take.

Soil: Peaty, well-drained loam.

Light: Able to grow in dimmer positions than most ferns.

Humidity: Although preferring reasonable humidity, they can thrive even in dry air conditions and do not mind draughts.

Watering: Must not be allowed to dry out – keep barely moist.

Feeding: Slow-release fertiliser sticks, granules or occasional organic liquid food during the growing season.

Propagation: Spores at any time or by division.

Uses: Ideal as specimen plants in pots or blended with other plants in indoor gardens.

Cyrtomium falcatum

Davallia bullata

Davallia varieties
Rabbit's foot fern

Habit: Davallias have dense foliage, light, ginger-coloured, hair-covered stems and rhizomes which curl over the edge of pots and baskets, adding interest to these charming ferns with their fine, dark green leaves like carrot tops.

Soil: A mixture of humus, peat moss or compost and river sand to improve drainage. Will also grow on moist bark or osmunda fibre.

Light: Happiest with good, indirect light near an east or west window.

Humidity: High humidity.

Watering: Keep moist during warmer months but drier during winter.

Feeding: Use a weak solution of organic liquid fertiliser every two months. Be careful of chemicals, especially on the leaves.

Propagation: Division or by pinning rhizomes to the soil until rooted.

Uses: Handsome basket subjects, with furry 'feet' growing over the edges of containers.

Varieties: There are a number of these including *D. canariensis* (deersfoot fern), but *D. trichomanoides,* also known as *D. bullata* (squirrel's foot fern), which has a longer leaf, is considered by many to be the best variety.

Microlepia speluncae

Microlepia speluncae

Habit: This Polynesian species has large leaves, each leaflet looking rather like a small feather.

Soil: Needs humus-rich soil, including peat moss which is capable of holding moisture. Grows under trees in nature.

Light: One of the few ferns that can take fairly dim light and is often found growing in caves, hence its Latin name *speluncae*.

Humidity: Growing even in fairly arid areas of Africa, it requires less humidity than most ferns.

Watering: Although they grow in dry areas in nature, it is usually in areas where water is easily accessible to their roots. Accordingly, the root balls should never be allowed to dry out when grown in pots.

Feeding: Use either a weak organic liquid solution occasionally, or slow-release fertiliser spikes or granules in the soil.

Propagation: By tissue culture or spores – best left to the professionals.

Uses: The ideal fern for low light positions where an airy, feathery look is required.

Nephrolepis exaltata
Sword fern

Habit: One of the most popular of indoor plants in Victorian times, this exuberant fern is still used a great deal because of its long leaves which arch on strong stems and cascade over the edges of pots or baskets. Today, however, many modern hybrids are generally seen in nurseries and garden centres.

Soil: Requires good loam enriched by peat moss or compost and a tablespoon of bone phosphate per bucketful. Include river sand at the bottom for good drainage.

Light: Unlike most ferns it can take some sun, but generally enjoys good indirect light. Some of the newer varieties, such as the compact *N. exaltata* 'Tuffii' can, however, tolerate poor light for short periods.

Humidity: Copes well even in dry climates, but does better with some humidity.

Watering: Keep barely moist.

Nephrolepis exaltata 'Boston Gold'

Below, left to right:
Nephrolepis exaltata 'Teddy Junior', 'Bostoniensis' and 'Whitmanii'

Feeding: Use either slow-release fertilisers or feed monthly with a liquid fertiliser. Do not, however, spray food on the leaves.

Propagation: By division. Grows so rapidly that it needs to be divided and repotted every few years. Creeping roots on the soil surface may also be cut off and planted out.

Uses: May be used for accent points, either cascading from large pots on pedestals or from baskets.

Varieties: There are a number of varieties but the best known and most popular is the Boston fern (*N. exaltata* 'Bostoniensis'). Its foliage is longer and more graceful than the common *N. exaltata*, and it forms a densely cascading plant with a softer appearance. A new variety, *N. exaltata* 'Boston Gold', is an excellent accent plant, with lovely pale yellow leaves dusted with gold. Two very compact varieties are *N. exaltata* 'Dallas', with dark green leaves and *N. exaltata* 'Tuffii'. Others include the more feathery varieties popular today such as *N. exaltata* 'Fluffy Ruffles' with fine fluffy foliage, *N. exaltata* 'Whitmanii' (lace fern); *N. exaltata* 'Teddy Junior'; *N. exaltata* 'Maassii' and *N. exaltata* 'Rooseveltii'.

Nephrolepis exaltata 'Maassii'

Pellaea rotundifolia

Pellaea rotundifolia
Button fern

Habit: This mini-fern from New Zealand is undoubtedly a plant with personality. It has small, round, button-like leaves on slender but strong, arching stems and is a dense, compact charmer few house plant lovers can resist. Its dark green leaves have a slightly leathery texture and are very different from those of most other plants. Small and rather round in form, and rarely growing taller than 20 cm, it is popular for use in areas which cannot take plants with large foliage.

Soil: A loose humus mixture with quantities of leaf mould.

Light: Can take reasonably poor light.

Humidity: Medium – thrives even in fairly dry regions.

Watering: Hates being soggy, but should never dry out or it might suffer a major setback from which it might not recover.

Feeding: Use liquid food monthly or the special slow-release fern fertilisers now available.

Propagation: By division or spores.

Uses: Ideal for use in small pots as mini-accent plants or as foreground fillers in groups or arrangements of plants.

Platycerium bifurcatum

Platycerium bifurcatum (immature)

Platycerium bifurcatum
Staghorn fern

Habit: These elegantly shaped epiphytic ferns of the rainforests adapt well indoors and have become popular house plants in South Africa as they can tolerate our generally dry inland and Highveld air. They grow on trees and rocks in nature, attaching themselves by means of sterile leaves which form shields. Indoors they grow well in airy, well-ventilated rooms on such mediums as bark or cork (see tip).

Soil: In nature they live on the humus formed by leaves and other dead organic material that collect behind their shields, but indoors they thrive on a finely sieved mixture of half compost and half peat moss.

Light: Good light to partial shade.

Humidity: High humidity; enjoy a soft spray of water occasionally.

Watering: Soak soil well and allow to dry out between waterings.

Feeding: Feed monthly during the growing season with liquid fertiliser. It is a good idea to immerse the entire bark section on which the plant grows into the fertiliser solution.

Propagation: By spores – this is best left to professionals. Should small plants develop at the side, these may be separated.

Uses: Their elegant leaves make them very decorative for use indoors.

Varieties: *P. bifurcatum* has generally been replaced today by an improved version which is very successful in the home, *P. alcicorne.*

TIP: The easiest way of attaching a staghorn fern to bark or cork is by pinning a square of small gauge chicken wire to your backing medium. Make a small slit from the centre of the top edge of the wire and open it in a V to form a pocket. Place some coir and sphagnum moss in the pocket and tuck some of your soil medium behind this. Ease in the roots of the plant and part of the shield before filling with the remaining soil. Make sure that the soil cannot be washed out when the plant is watered. Arrange the rest of the shield so that it is outside the wire and allow its 'antlers' to hang free in front. As the plant grows and shields develop, the wire will be totally hidden. Plants may also be attached in a similar manner by means of pantihose.

Pteris varieties
Table fern

Habit: A wide variety of these plants is used as house plants today and with their strange but distinctive, lance-like leaves – some plain green and some variegated with cream or white – they give a light, airy feel, particularly when used with other plants. They do not enjoy hot positions.

Soil: Loose humus soil.

Light: Suitable for bright to medium bright positions – no sun.

Humidity: Enjoy high humidity – best kept on a humidity tray.

Watering: Keep moist at all times. If dry, the leaves go brown and look burnt. If this happens, remove the leaves and wait for new growth.

Feeding: Feed regularly with liquid food at half-strength from spring to autumn, tailing off in winter.

Propagation: By plant division and spores.

Uses: Attractive used alone, but especially suited to enlivening plant arrangements.

Varieties: *P. ensiformis* 'Evergemensis' is a charming, small fern, growing no more than 0,5 m tall. It has striking leaves with silver centres. *P. ensiformis* 'Victoriae' has a silvery-white midrib. Other varieties include *P. cretica*, known as ribbon fern; a variegated form, *P. cretica* 'Albo-lineata', which has a creamy-white central stripe; *P. cretica* 'Parkerii', small and compact with shiny green leaves and broad, finely toothed leaflets; and *P. cretica* 'Roewerii', similar to 'Parkerii' but with frillier leaves. *P. tremula*, with lovely yellow-green leaves, is a fine table plant when small, but later needs floor space. *P. cretica* 'Mayi' has leaves with a gold central stripe and frayed tips.

Pteris cretica 'Roewerii'

Pteris cretica 'Albo-lineata'

Pteris ensiformis 'Evergemensis'

Pteris cretica 'Mayi'

6. *Palms*

Arecastrum romanzoffianum

Arecastrum romanzoffianum (Cocos plumosa)

Queen palm

Habit: A very tall palm in nature, this lovely plant eventually grows too tall for most homes and may then be transferred to the garden. Indoors it may be used as a striking addition to rooms where height is needed. It is a quick grower, and has arching stems which are held more or less upright when young, but long trailing leaflets give it a soft, feathery appearance.

Soil: Use a mixture of equal parts garden soil, compost and river sand, and ensure good drainage with a layer of river sand at the bottom of the pot.

Light: Provide with the best light possible and preferably some sunlight.

Humidity: Average.

Watering: Water well and then allow the surface to dry before watering again.

Feeding: Use organic liquid fertiliser once a month.

Propagation: Seed.

Uses: Seen to best effect in atriums, double-volume rooms and well-lit stairwells.

Chamaedorea elegans (Neanthe bella)

Parlour palm

Habit: These are slow-growing, but extremely attractive palms even when small and are sold in shops as love palms. They are single-stemmed miniatures with spiralling leaves and rarely grow to more than 1,2 m in a container. Even when small they produce attractive, orange, date-like fruits. Chamaedoreas enjoy fitting snugly into their pots and are unhappy when overpotted.

Soil: Commercial potting soil is ideal provided it drains well. Ensure that there is a good layer of river sand for drainage at the bottom of the pot.

Light: Used to growing on the floor of the forest in nature, chamaedoreas are able to take fairly dim and even stuffy conditions, making them ideal for air-conditioned offices.

Humidity: Normal.

Watering: Keep moist but not damp. They hate soggy conditions or having to stand in a saucer filled with water.

Feeding: Chamaedoreas enjoy regular feeding with diluted liquid food during the spring and summer growing period.

Propagation: By seed, but it is not easy and must be done under extremely humid conditions.

Uses: An ideal palm for virtually any indoor situation short of direct sunlight. It always looks neat and is so compact that when small it makes an ideal terrarium subject.

> **TIP:** Three *Chamaedorea elegans* plants grouped together in a bowl make a most attractive arrangement for office desk tops. Avoid using chemical cleaners on the leaves as they are easily damaged.

Chamaedorea elegans

Chamaedorea seifritzii

Chamaedorea seifritzii
Reed palm

Habit: Ideal for providing height without too much density, this multi-stemmed variety grows suckers which form clumps of slender, reed-like stems topped by attractive, slightly stiff, pinnate (feather-like) leaves. Leaflets are generally slender but the end pair open slightly larger than the rest, giving the appearance of a whale's tail. Cut back less attractive stems occasionally to encourage fresh growth.

Soil: Enjoys a well-drained mixture which should be aerated with one third or more organic matter like compost and humus, as well as some river sand.

Light: One of the better choices for dim positions, but will also thrive in well-lit areas, provided it gets no direct sun.

Humidity: Average.

Watering: Keep on the dry side rather than wet. Allow the surface of the potting mixture to dry before soaking well.

Feeding: Do not overfeed. It is best to use a slow-release feed such as plant sticks or powder. Alternatively, use a liquid food once a quarter.

Propagation: By seed or division of suckers.

Uses: Very much a decorator's plant with lovely lines.

Varieties: *C. microspadix,* another multi-stemmed palm, is similar to *C. seifritzii* in many ways. Its stems are, however, more slender and the leaves less erect. It makes a fine tub specimen but is not yet easily available in South Africa.

Chrysalidocarpus lutescens
Bamboo palm

Habit: Though known as the bamboo palm in South Africa, this beautiful specimen or accent plant is known overseas by a number of names, including golden feather and butterfly palm. Golden feather is probably the best description, for it produces masses of feathery fronds from a dense bamboo-like cluster of stems. 'Lutescens' means yellow and this refers to the palm's slender golden stems. Indoors the leaves are generally a delightful soft green, but out of doors and even in a very sunny window they too are yellow. This Madagascan beauty reaches 3 m indoors and needs a lot of space for its lovely arching branches. The leaves must be sponged down regularly to remove dust. It enjoys air circulation.

Soil: Include at least one third organic matter in the soil mix and ensure good drainage with a layer of river sand at the base of the pot and some mixed into the soil. Refresh the soil annually and repot into a pot one size larger every second year.

Light: Provide as much sun as possible and bright light for the rest of the day. North windows are ideal.

Humidity: Average.

Watering: Be careful not to overwater. Allow the surface to dry out before irrigating again.

Feeding: Overfeeding causes leaf tips to turn brown – give liquid fertiliser only every quarter.

Propagation: Best done by seed, but really a job for the professionals.

Uses: Having a lovely soft, flowing appearance, they are well suited to decorate living rooms, walkways and entrance halls. They also make fine office plants if given a bright, sunny situation.

Chrysalidocarpus lutescens

Cocos nucifera

Cocos nucifera
Coconut palm

Habit: This is probably the plant that jumps to mind when most people think of the tropics or South Sea islands. In nature it produces one of the largest fronds of any palm and is very much a novelty in the home. It needs to be moved out of the house when it starts to form mature leaves and in sub-tropical areas it may be planted into the garden with success. Fortunately it is a slow grower and does not mind being potbound. As a result it has recently become the darling of interior decorators in Europe and America and is now becoming popular as an indoor patio plant in South Africa. Adding to its charm as a young plant, it grows from the large nut itself, and provides striking silhouettes when grown in a large bowl. Initially sold in either 22 cm or 30 cm pots, it will need to be repotted into larger pots of 30 cm and 35 cm respectively after a year.

Soil: Requires quick-draining and well-aerated soil, such as commercial potting soil, otherwise blend equal parts of good garden loam, compost and river sand.

Light: This must be as bright as possible and the plant should ideally be placed near a north window. Increase the light if the leaves turn yellow.

Humidity: Average, but in dry areas it enjoys having its leaves misted from time to time.

Watering: Needs to be watered at least twice a week – it must be kept on the damp side, but not soggy.

Feeding: Needs very little food. Initially the palm feeds off the nut, so it is unnecessary to feed it for many months. As it matures, it does best with a slow-release fertiliser such as a food spike, though it will appreciate foliar feed spray every three to four months.

Propagation: This is best done from the nut when the sprout forces its way through one of the three eyes at the top of the nut, hence its name 'coco', the Portuguese word for a grimace. Propagation is, however, basically a job for the professional horticulturist.

Uses: Ideal for use on low tables or broad windowsills. They are particularly attractive on stoep or patio tables or near a swimming pool.

Howea forsteriana (Kentia forsteriana)
Sentry palm

Habit: The kentia, as it is usually, though incorrectly, known, is one of the least temperamental of palms and among the best plants for dim positions where height is needed. Growing to 3 m, it has large leaves with slightly trailing leaflets arching from a single stem.

Soil: The ideal mix is 50 per cent good garden loam, 25 per cent peat moss or sieved compost and 25 per cent river sand.

Light: Needs little light, for in its natural state it survives in the deepest shade of the Pacific forests.

Humidity: Has above average requirements, being used to sultry heat, yet surprisingly it can survive in icy air-conditioning.

Watering: The surface of the soil should dry between waterings.

Feeding: Use organic liquid food quarterly.

Propagation: Seeds.

Uses: Ideal for offices, modern and period homes, it is especially useful where height is needed in stairwells or double-volume rooms.

Varieties: *H. belmoreana* is very similar but has smaller, more upright leaves and grows to about half the height of *H. forsteriana.*

Howea forsteriana

Phoenix roebelenii

Phoenix roebelenii
Miniature date palm

Habit: One of the most popular of the small palms, it is unlikely to top a metre indoors, except in the most perfect conditions, such as a very light, airy position. It has a dense crown of graceful, arching leaves, with narrow, attractive, dark green leaflets, which initially seem to spring from the ground but slowly lift on a very slender stem.

Soil: Like all palms, it needs a light soil containing at least one third humus and some river sand to ensure good drainage. Commercial potting soil may be used, but if it is fairly heavy improve it with additional organic material.

Light: *P. roebelenii* needs at least four hours of sun a day and should be kept in a position where it is able to enjoy light practically all day. It should have a bright window position where there is plenty of air movement.

Humidity: Medium.

Watering: Keep moist but not wet. Never allow to dry out completely. Drench thoroughly and allow to drain before replacing in its container. Water sparingly in winter, using the finger test method to discover when this is necessary.

Feeding: Feed with liquid fertiliser fortnightly.

Propagation: Seeds.

Uses: When young, *P. roebelenii* may be used on low tables or even as a centrepiece on a large table. As it gets bigger it makes an excellent floor subject and deserves a very elegant brass or ceramic pot.

TIP: Palms enjoy bright positions with plenty of air movement and should have their leaves sponged regularly or gently hosed down outdoors. They will benefit from being put into the garden occasionally, particularly if it is raining. When away on holiday, place your palms in a shady spot under trees – they will reward you with better growth if you do.

Rhapis excelsa

Rhapis excelsa
Lady palm

Habit: A bushy palm with dense stem clusters, this slow grower is very hardy and an ideal container plant for indoor conditions. It has fan-like, ribbed leaves, each segment being almost separate from its neighbour, and its tips are slightly square rather than pointed. The base of its stiff, bamboo-like stem is covered with coarse fibres. Indoors it rarely grows to more than 1,5 m.

Soil: Best grown in a mixture of equal parts soil, compost and river sand.

Light: Will grow in reasonably dim areas but does best in brighter positions, near a north or east window.

Humidity: Medium.

Watering: Soak thoroughly and then allow the surface to dry before watering again.

Feeding: Apply organic liquid fertiliser once a month.

Propagation: Division or seed.

Uses: An excellent floor subject in living rooms, studies and offices. It looks good in a large basket.

7. Succulents and cacti

Aeonium arboreum 'Nigrum'

Aeonium arboreum 'Nigrum'
Zwartkop

Habit: Rosettes of glossy, purple-black leaves are a feature of this striking indigenous plant. It is at its most attractive when the stems are short and the plant is compact.

Soil: Include some river sand in a rich loam soil mixture, to ensure good drainage. Add 25 per cent mushroom compost to poor soil.

Light: Strong light, preferably direct sun is needed to maintain the plant's condition, otherwise it may drop its leaves or rosettes. The more sun it gets, the darker its leaves become.

Humidity: Low.

Watering: Water well once a week, then leave to dry.

Feeding: None necessary unless the plant is pot-bound.

Propagation: Multiplies easily; plant out the main rosettes and the small ones that form on the sides of old stems.

Uses: An attractive plant for sunny windowsills.

TIP: Unattractive once it becomes leggy, a good idea is to cut off each rosette, retaining just a short length of stem and replanting it.

Agave victoriae-reginae
Queen agave

Habit: Like other members of this Mexican genus, it forms dense rosettes of leaves. They are about 20 cm long and dark green with beautiful white markings and stubby, spiny tips.

Soil: Add one third river sand to commercial potting soil to ensure good drainage and enrich it with 25 per cent mushroom compost.

Light: As much sunlight as possible and the best light.

Humidity: Dry.

Watering: Limited water, but more during the active summer growth season than during winter.

Feeding: None necessary.

Propagation: From seed only.

Uses: A good pot specimen.

Varieties: *A. filifera* has a small, stiff rosette of green leaves tipped with white. *A. parviflora* is also a small-growing variety with fine, wispy threads at the leaf tips.

Agave victoriae-reginae

Cephalocereus senilis

Cephalocereus senilis
Old man cactus

Habit: The entire plant is covered in long white hair, hence its very apt common name. Columnar in shape, it may grow to 10 m or more in nature, but it is nevertheless an excellent indoor plant because of its extremely slow growth rate. It rarely grows taller than 0,5 m indoors. Handle with care as its hair conceals sharp spines.

Soil: Add one third river sand to a commercial soil mix to ensure good drainage. Also add 25 per cent well-rotted mushroom compost.

Light: Must have direct sun, or filtered sunlight all day.

Humidity: Dry.

Watering: Water well, then allow it to dry before watering again. These plants rot easily if overwatered.

Feeding: None necessary.

Propagation: By seeds or tip cuttings in late spring. Allow cuttings to form calluses before placing them on top of a sandy soil mix to root.

Uses: An excellent pot specimen for height.

TIP: If the white hair of your old man cactus becomes dirty or matted, give it a shampoo with a mild solution of soapy water. Rinse off immediately with clean water and allow it to dry in the sun. Then comb neatly.

Ceropegia woodii (Ceropegia linearis)
String of hearts

Habit: Known by many names, including hearts entwined and rosary vine, this charming member of the succulent family is a tiny trailing plant with mottled green and silver miniature heart-shaped leaves, arranged in pairs on long thread-like stems which can reach 75 cm. One of the easiest of house plants, it is at its best when grown in hanging baskets which show up the purple undersides of the leaves. It grows quickly, from tiny bulbs which store water, and it occasionally produces small, lantern-shaped flowers.

Soil: Needs a fairly rich, loam-based soil mix which includes some peat moss, a little well-dried kraal manure and some crushed charcoal. An ideal subject for the hydroponic growing method.

Light: Ceropegias enjoy a lot of light and do well on sunny windowsills where their long stems can hang down the wall.

Humidity: Ceropegias prefer dry air and thrive in most inland areas, but also grow reasonably well on hot windowsills in humid coastal areas.

Watering: Requiring little water, particularly in winter, ceropegias should be allowed to dry out before being re-watered.

Feeding: During summer, feed occasionally with a diluted solution of liquid fertiliser.

Propagation: Place leaves with a piece of stem in a pot containing peat moss or divide the bulblets.

Uses: Ideal as a decoration for windowsills, room dividers and bookcases, or for use in small baskets where it can hang down but still be seen at eye-level.

Ceropegia woodii

Echeveria derenbergii

Echeveria derenbergii
Painted lady

Habit: Rosette-forming, with succulent blue-grey leaves which are slightly frosted with red-tinged tips and margins, this is one of the best of an attractive genus. During summer, each plant produces many spikes of small yellow, bell-like flowers that force their way between its leaves.

Soil: Use commercial potting soil to which at least one third river sand and some mushroom compost have been added.

Light: Sunshine for at least part of the day, otherwise bright light.

Humidity: Low.

Watering: Should almost dry out between waterings.

Feeding: None necessary.

Propagation: Planting offsets or rosettes is easiest, but seed and leaf cuttings are also successful.

Uses The ideal pot plant for a hot, sunny window.

Varieties: There are a number of these, but among the prettiest is *E.* 'Doris Taylor', which is similar to *E. derenbergii,* but with leaves covered in fine, silver hairs. *E. setosa* also has slightly hairy leaves, but these hug the ground more closely than other varieties.

Echinopsis varieties
Sea urchin cactus

Habit: Globular in form, though elongating with age, these cacti are notable for their attractive, scented flowers which, after an initial flush at the start of summer, continue spasmodically throughout the hot months. Although early flowers grow close to the plant, stems tend to lengthen into tubes as the plant ages. Flowers of 10 cm wide start opening at dusk and fade the following day.

Soil: Use equal parts river sand, commercial potting soil and well-rotted mushroom compost.

Light: Must have several hours of direct sun each day and bright light for the rest of the day.

Humidity: As low as possible.

Watering: Allow the plant to dry out between deep waterings and provide with considerably less moisture during the cool months.

Feeding: None necessary.

Propagation: Each spring, plant out offsets from the mass formed at the base of the plants.

Uses: An excellent choice for a tray garden or as a lone pot plant in a sunny windowsill.

Varieties: *E. multiplex,* the best known of the genus, forms a pale green, barrel-shaped stem, ribbed with round clusters of strong, brown, needle-like spines. It produces fragrant, pale pink blooms. Modern hybrids of this plant have day-flowering orange, red and yellow blooms. *E. eyriesii* has a darker barrel with scented white flowers.

Below and bottom: *Echinopsis multiplex* varieties

Euphorbia milii splendens

Euphorbia varieties

Habit: This is a large plant genus of varied forms and manners of flowering, and includes the cactus-like *E. horrida* and *E. mammillaria,* the tree-like candelabra *E. pseudocactus,* the more shrub-like *E. fulgens* and the Christ's-thorn, *E. milii splendens.* All of these make good house plants if given sufficient sun and light.

Soil: Good drainage is vital. Use a mixture of equal parts river sand, commercial potting soil and mushroom compost.

Light: Very good light is needed with at least four or five hours of sun.

Humidity: Dry.

Watering: Many euphorbias come from summer rainfall areas and should be kept reasonably well watered during summer, but never soggy. In winter use only sufficient water to prevent shrivelling.

Feeding: None necessary unless the plant becomes potbound.

Propagation: By seeds and cuttings (see tip below).

Uses: Most euphorbias, being rather large, are best used in sunny areas where space is not a problem.

Varieties: These include: *E. burmanii,* small but boldly branching with clusters of green flowers at the tips of twisting stems; *E. bupleurifolis,* which has strange knobbly stems with sparse but quaintly attractive leaves at the tips and produces small yellow-green flowers in spring, and the popular cow's thorn *(E. grandicornis),* a rather awkwardly branched and segmented variety with potent 6 cm long spines.

TIP: When taking a euphorbia cutting, always wash it in water immediately to prevent the milk which flows from the wound from forming a scab. Then allow the clean cutting to dry in a cool place for two weeks. Once planted in a mixture of half river sand and half peat moss, your cutting will start growing almost immediately. It is, however, extremely difficult to develop a new plant from a cutting on which a milk scab has formed.

Kalanchoe tomentosa
Panda plant

Habit: This plant has pale green leaves resembling panda paws. They are covered in fluffy, white hairs and have prominent paw markings, which are rusty brown when young and darken with age. The leaves form attractive but stiff rosettes on upright stems, varying in height from 25-40 cm. The leaves have a felt-like feel to them.

Soil: Equal parts potting soil, river sand and mushroom compost.

Light: Requires excellent light and preferably a few hours of sun, otherwise it is inclined to become leggy.

Humidity: Dry.

Watering: Allow to dry between deep waterings.

Feeding: None necessary.

Propagation: Tip and leaf cuttings planted in a mixture of peat moss and river sand.

Uses: Attractive in any sunny window, but particularly in children's rooms, who love them.

Varieties: There are a number of kalanchoes, but two popular varieties are *K. beharensis* with large, felt-like, grey-green leaves on strong, upright stems and *K. pumila,* with fine, powder-covered, pink-grey leaves which tend to trail.

Kalanchoe tomentosa

Lithops pseudotruncatella

Lithops bella

Lithops varieties
Pebble plants

Habit: Often called living stones due to their remarkable similarity to pebbles, our indigenous lithops are formed of pairs of thick, succulent and fleshy leaves which lie flat on the ground. Mixed with real pebbles, they are barely distinguishable. Some have a marbled appearance while others are plain. All send out a flower – often larger than the plant itself – through a slit-like fissure which divides the plant, either in late summer or autumn. A few varieties form clumps.

Soil: Equal parts commercial potting soil, washed river sand and well-rotted mushroom compost. Enjoy a clay-based soil.

Light: As much sun and bright light as possible.

Humidity: Dry.

Watering: Water once every two weeks in winter and once a week in summer.

Feeding: None necessary.

Propagation: Those varieties that form clumps, by division; others by seed.

Uses: Lithops are ideal plants for a pebble tray arrangement. Try to collect a variety of these rather attractive curiosities – they're marvellous talking points.

Varieties: There are a number, but two of the best are the clump-forming *L. bella,* with silver-grey leaves and fragrant white blooms, and *L. fulleri,* with brown markings on pale, grey-green leaves and white flowers. Yellow flowering forms include *L. lesliei; L. aucampii* and *L. pseudotruncatella.*

TIP: Do not be alarmed when, after flowering, your lithops starts to shrivel and appears to be dying. This is normal and you will find late in spring that two new leaves emerge from the shrivelled parent shell. Do not water the plant during the withering period.

Mammillaria varieties

Habit: Probably the most common forms of cactus seen in the home because of the charming, fluffy, powder-puff-like shapes, and circlets of flowers like garlands in a girl's hair. Small-growing, they are extremely popular with children. They are ribless, and most of them are covered in symmetrically placed tufts of spines, hairs or hooks and have a deceptively soft appearance. Some appear as single barrels, while others form clusters of globular plants in varying sizes.

Soil: Add half a cup of bone phosphate to each bucket of soil mix, made up of a blend of potting soil, river sand and mushroom compost in equal parts.

Light: Mammillarias need bright light and do best where they get about half a day's sun daily or filtered sunlight all day.

Humidity: Low.

Watering: Water deeply and then leave until almost dry.

Feeding: Quarterly with organic liquid fertiliser.

Propagation: By separating plantlets from the mother plant.

Uses: Extremely decorative, and ideal for sunny window-sills anywhere, particularly in children's rooms.

Varieties: There are hundreds of varieties of this genus but among the most popular are: *M. speciosa*, the spring-flowering nipple cactus; *M. spinosissima*, which is globular with reddish-purple flowers; *M. gracilis*, a small clump-forming variety, which multiplies rapidly; *M. parkinsonii*, or owl's eyes, a summer-flowering, clump-forming, ball-like cactus; *M. elongata*, a small-growing cluster of slightly elongated plantlets of varying height but never much taller than 10 cm and with a lace-like covering of tiny barbs; *M. bocasana*, the snowball cactus, which lives up to its name by being entirely covered in silver hairs, except at its top where there is a circlet in which flowers form; and *M. hahniana*, covered in white, hair-like bristles which are responsible for its common name, old lady cactus.

TIP: Examine all cacti with a dense covering of hair and spines for mealy bug. These pests can be a problem, often sucking sap from the plant without your realising it. If discovered, treat with a systemic insecticide.

Mammillaria spinosissima

Rebutia senilis

Rebutia calliantha
Crown cactus

Habit: A tiny plant but a prolific flowerer in spring and early summer. This species of cactus generally grows to no more than 10 cm high, forming clusters of plants. The ball-like little plants are most attractive and produce circlets of bright orange flowers. Tiny spines generally spread out in a whirlpool design from the top centre. In South Africa the rebutias, particularly the very small varieties, are often seen grafted onto stems of other cactus varieties and are much sought after.

Soil: An easy-draining, well-aerated, humus-based soil which includes one third river sand, and one third mushroom compost.

Light: A high degree of light, including as much sun as possible.

Humidity: Low.

Watering: Water deeply, then allow to dry out before watering again.

Feeding: None necessary.

Propagation: By separating plantlets when repotting your plant every second year and by seed.

Uses: For colour on sunny windowsills. A must for any collection and excellent for tray gardens.

Varieties: *R. albiflora,* a very small variety with white flowers; *R. krainsiana* with beautiful orange flowers; and *R. senilis,* which has red flowers with silvery-white spines and is a great producer of clumps of attractive offsets.

TIP: Use stout leather gloves when handling even the most innocent looking cactus. Many are covered in fine hair and appear to be quite harmless but underneath are often a multitude of vicious barbs.

Sansevieria varieties
Mother-in-law's tongue

Habit: Easy to grow, these tough indigenous plants with tall, erect, sword-like leaves thrive under practically any conditions, but under ideal conditions, including the correct soil mixture, they are superb. Almost a metre tall, they have slightly wavy leaves, some of which are margined, some banded.

Soil: A coarse, well-composted, well-drained, pebbly soil.

Light: Can take low light, but are at their best when grown in bright light with some sun. Will also grow with eight hours of artificial light per day.

Humidity: Low.

Watering: Water moderately during the warmer months, and allow to dry out between waterings, but keep dryish during winter. Spots on leaves indicate overwatering.

Feeding: Fertilise only during summer, with a strength below that recommended for general indoor plants.

Propagation: Rhizomes divide easily at any time of the year. May also be grown from cuttings, but these produce only green plants. Repotting is only necessary when pots become completely overcrowded.

Uses: Sansevierias are one of the toughest and easiest-to-grow house plants available. They are so adaptable that they may be grown virtually anywhere and are ideal for those dim places where few other plants will survive. They are strikingly decorative where upright accent is required. Several planted into a large pot make excellent specimen plants when standing on the floor or on a low table. They also look good in Victorian settings.

Varieties: *S. trifasciata,* the most popular form, has silver-grey leaves with darker green, horizontal bands. *S. trifasciata* 'Hahnii' is a miniature version of *S. trifasciata* with similar markings but shorter, stubbier leaves which form a funnel. *S. trifasciata* 'Laurentii' has grey-green leaves outlined with broad yellow edges. One variety, known as mother-in-law's toothpicks or spear sansevieria, has cylindrical leaves tapering to points which are cross-banded with dark green and yellow-green.

Sansevieria trifasciata 'Laurentii'

Sedum morganianum

Sedum morganianum
Burro's tail

Habit: This plant's trailing stems are densely covered with the typically jelly bean-like leaves of the *Sedum* genus. Stems, 50 cm or more long, grow very densely and eventually form a very full basket with strong eye appeal, for the blue-green colour of the leaves is most attractive.

Soil: Mix one part river sand, one part commercial potting soil and one part mushroom compost.

Light: As much sunlight as possible, and is best hanging on a bright stoep with morning or afternoon sun.

Humidity: Low.

Watering: Water well during the growing period but allow the surface to dry out to a depth of about one centimetre before watering again. During winter allow to dry even deeper before watering again.

Feeding: None necessary.

Propagation: Best done with short stem cuttings during spring and summer. Remove sufficient leaves from the growing end to insert the stem into the soil. Leave to dry for a day or two before placing in a sandy growing medium.

Uses: Extremely attractive, and is ideal for decorating sunny windows or bright stoeps and patios.

TIP: To create an attractive, full effect it is best to grow several plantlets together in a hanging bowl. Be careful to place it in an area where it is easy to water, but where you are unlikely to knock it as the leaflets fall off easily.

Sedum rubrotinctum
Jelly bean plant

Habit: Clusters of upright stems are densely covered with succulent, fleshy, green leaves like jelly beans tipped with red, hence this charming plant's common name. It occasionally produces yellow flowers.

Soil: One part river sand, one part commercial potting soil and one part mushroom compost.

Light: Thrives best on sunny windowsills. Low light will impair colour.

Humidity: Low.

Watering: During the growing season water well and then allow to dry out. In winter water only enough to prevent shrivelling. The drier the conditions, the more colourful the plants.

Feeding: None necessary except for pot-bound plants.

Propagation: By 8 cm long stem cuttings. Strip off the lower leaves before inserting the stems into a soil mix of half potting soil, half sand.

Uses: For colour on windowsills or stoep tables.

TIP: This plant is most attractive when stems of roughly the same height are clustered. Remove any leggy stems to keep your plant bushy. Best grown in wide bowls to allow for space to spread.

Sedum rubrotinctum

Senecio rowleyanus

Senecio rowleyanus
String of pearls

Habit: Namibia's popular succulent trailer, also known as the bead vine, is a real winner. So named because of the charming way its bead-shaped leaves cling to long trailing stems of 60 cm or more, it is not only attractive but one of the easiest house plants to grow. In addition to its blue-green, small, round leaves with a tiny 'window' at the top, this senecio produces minute, dandelion-like flowers if it has sufficient light.

Soil: Use a humus mixture which includes about one third river sand, one third potting soil and one third mushroom compost. Repot every two or three years.

Light: Needs a lot of light and will do well on any sunny windowsill.

Humidity: Although it enjoys low humidity, this plant seems to thrive in most regions of South Africa.

Watering: Water well and leave until almost dry before watering again.

Feeding: None necessary.

Propagation: From seed or cuttings.

Uses: Excellent trailing from small pots on a mantelpiece, fridge or bookshelves, and from hanging pots.

Varieties: *S. herreianus,* often called the gooseberry plant, is very similar to the plant described above, except that its beads are larger.

Zygocactus truncatus

Zygocactus truncatus (Schlumbergera truncata)

Habit: Unlike most cacti, this variety, known as the holiday cactus in the USA, requires some shade. However, it will thrive indoors if hung in a sunny window. With many segmented, flat, pendulous branches, it produces masses of multi-layered and frilled flowers at the end of each drooping stem in midwinter.

Soil: One part river sand, one part commercial potting soil and one part well-rotted mushroom compost.

Light: Being a forest cactus rather than a desert variety, it can take medium light, although it needs bright light during the blooming period (see tip below).

Humidity: Higher than normal for cacti - about 25 per cent.

Watering: Should be kept reasonably moist, although the surface may dry out slightly. Needs more water when budding and flowering, and also during the active growing period in spring.

Feeding: Use liquid fertiliser fortnightly during the budding and flowering period, but feed only monthly for the rest of the year.

Propagation: Stems with two or more segments root rapidly in spring. Allow the stems to dry out and form calluses for a few days before inserting them into the soil.

Varieties: The zygocactus has been hybridised to produce a great many differently coloured flowers, from white to pink, rose, red, salmon and purple. Very similar to and often also called zygocactus, is the *Schlumbergera gaertneri,* which may be distinguished from its look-alike by the fact that its segmented leaves have less prominently serrated edges.

TIP: Zygocactus are short-day plants and need naturally short days during autumn if they are to flower properly. So during this period preceding their flowering it is best to keep them in an area where they are not troubled by electric light at night, otherwise they will become confused and will not bloom. Once flowering, night light does not matter.

Index

Numbers in **bold** type indicate main plant entries; * after a page number indicates an illustration

Photographic credits

Photographs by John Brunda © 1988 Human & Rousseau (Pty.) Ltd.:
p. 2; p. 12; p. 14; p. 17; p. 20; p. 28 (top, right; bottom, second from left; and bottom, extreme right); p. 29 (top; and bottom, second from left); p. 30 (right); p. 32; p. 34 (left); p. 35 (right); p. 37; p. 39 (left, top and bottom); p. 40 (left, top and bottom; and bottom, right); p. 40/41 (bottom); p. 41 (bottom, left; and top, left); p. 43 (top); p. 45; p. 46 (top, left); p. 47 (right); p. 48 (top); p. 49; p.50 (left; and right, top); p. 53; p. 54; p. 55; p. 56; p. 58; p. 59 (right); p. 60; p. 61; p. 62; p. 63; p. 64; p. 65; p. 66; p. 68; p. 69; p. 71; p. 72 (bottom); p. 74 (bottom, left); p. 75 (top, left); p. 78; p. 79; p. 80; p. 81; p. 82; p. 83; p. 84; p. 85; p. 86 (left, bottom; and right, top); p. 87 (top, right); p. 88; p. 89; p. 90 (bottom, right); p. 91; p. 92; p. 93 (top, right); p. 94 (left); p. 95; p. 96; p. 97; p. 98; p. 99; p. 100; p. 101 (bottom, right); p. 102; p. 103; p. 104; p. 105 (top, right); p. 106; p. 107; p. 108; p. 109 (right); p. 110; p. 111; p. 112 (top, left and right); p. 113; p. 114; p. 116; p. 117; p. 118; p. 119; p. 120 (right); p. 121; p. 123 (bottom, right); p. 124; p. 125; p. 126; p. 127; p. 128; p. 129; p. 130 (bottom, right); p. 132 (bottom, right); p. 136 (left); p. 137 (right); p. 138

Photographs by Rob Böck © 1988 Human & Rousseau (Pty.) Ltd.:
p. 43 (bottom); p. 44 (top); p. 51; p. 72 (top); p. 73 (top, left); p. 130 (top, left); p. 131 (right, top and bottom); p. 132 (top, left); p. 133; p. 134; p. 135

Photographs and copyright © 1988 Nancy Gardiner:
p. 8; p. 10; p. 11; p. 28 (bottom, extreme left); p. 29 (bottom, extreme left; second from right; and extreme right); p. 31; p. 33; p. 34 (right); p. 35 (left); p. 36; p. 38; p. 39 (bottom, right); p. 41 (bottom, right); p. 42 (top); p. 46 (bottom, right); p. 47 (left); p. 48 (bottom); p. 52; p. 57 (left, top and right); p. 59 (left); p. 67; p. 70; p. 73 (right, top and bottom); p. 74 (top, right); p. 75 (bottom, right); p. 76; p. 77; p. 86 (right, centre and bottom); p. 87 (left, top and bottom); p. 90 (top, left); p. 93 (bottom, left); p. 101 (top, left); p. 105 (bottom, left); p. 120 (left); p. 123 (top, left); p. 131 (top, left); p. 136/137 (centre); p. 139

Photograph and copyright © 1988 C. Kunhardt:
p. 50 (right, bottom)

Photographs by John Brunda © 1988 Owen A. Reid:
p. 19; p. 22; p. 28 (top, left; and bottom, second from right); p. 30 (left; and centre, top); p. 40 (top, right); p. 42 (bottom); p. 44 (bottom); p. 57 (left, bottom); p. 94 (right); p. 109 (left); p. 112 (bottom, right); p. 115; p. 122

Photographs on cover by John Brunda © 1988 Human & Rousseau except photograph of asparagus fern on front cover by Nancy Gardiner